ROBERT T SMITH

Robert T Smith
Revisited

StarTribune Columnist 1968–1989

NODIN PRESS
MINNEAPOLIS

Copyright 1997, Star Tribune.
Republished with permission.
Star Tribune retains all copyright and syndication rights.

All rights reserved. No part of this book may be reproduced
in any form without the permission of Nodin Press
except for review purposes.

ISBN 0-931714-76-1.

NODIN PRESS
a division of Micawber's Inc.
525 North Third Street
Minneapolis, MN 55401

First printing

I would like to dedicate this book to all my readers during the 21 years of doing my column, first for The Minneapolis Tribune *and then for the* Star Tribune. *Without those readers, it wouldn't have been possible. I chose to write about real people, most of whom were unknown. It was the reader who supplied me with leads for many of those columns. The reader knew what I wanted. And then, more specifically, I would like to dedicate the book also to Clara Landvik, my sixth-grade teacher. I had written a few things in her class. One day, she took me aside and said: "Robert you can't spell cat, but you have a talent for writing." No one had said that to me before. It stuck in my mind and I decided that I would one day try to be a professional writer.*

TABLE OF CONTENTS

9 Foreword *Jon Hassler*
11 Introduction *Robert T. Smith*

COLUMNS 1968–1989

25	Wait for my second term	November 22, 1968
26	A touch of white stuff in New York	January 8, 1969
27	Stripper Gypsy is a knitter	April 28, 1970
28	No one wants her anymore	September 20, 1970
29	Berryman: Indifference never came	January 9, 1972
30	Someone going really nowhere	April 10, 1972
30	Butterflies are chasing her now	March 10, 1974
31	A picturesque divorce	March 28, 1974
32	A visit by hypocrisy	November 17, 1974
33	Jack Benny: a terrible beginner	December 29, 1974
34	He relied on imagination and humor	January 2, 1975
35	A bewildered boy gets help	February 2, 1975
36	Without a book, she felt naked	March 23, 1975
37	Danny Kaye: laughs for sick kids	May 5, 1975
38	The buzzards at least are honest	August 13, 1975
39	She wanted to die alone . . .	August 19, 1975
39	A doctor for all reasons	September 15, 1975
41	Lilli Palmer, fragile, quiet and beautiful	October 16, 1975
42	He pleads guilty with pleasure	January 10, 1976
43	A hug for a different little girl	February 2, 1976
43	Glen Olson: the impractical joker	April 12, 1976
45	URIS—absurd actors on diabolical stage	June 22, 1976
46	Poetic Bus Driver: "Don't fall on the mall"	July 2, 1976
47	He laughed and smiled a lot—and yet . . .	August 17, 1976
48	A wino with a heart	January 3, 1977
49	For 21 years, a secret admirer	May 29, 1977
50	He can't forgive . . . yet	September 11, 1977
51	And now, a rock and a cloud to go	September 14, 1977
52	The definition of a reporter	December 4, 1977
53	Place an anise bag around your neck	November 22, 1978
55	Pete: Master of the pun	December 20, 1978
56	John Gutowski—Mr. Auditorium	December 24, 1978
57	They really want Christmas to end	December 25, 1978

ROBERT T SMITH

58	Smiths: Never a president	January 17, 1979
59	A. J.—he ministers a bus	April 6, 1979
60	Jerome Hines: his voice is on the bums	May 14, 1979
61	10 or 20 little orange things	May 16, 1979
61	The end of the downtown characters	May 20, 1979
62	For a little boy: nothing impossible	May 23, 1979
63	The Little Wagon—a third place	June 6, 1979
64	She died after returning from Oz	November 7, 1979
66	"I wear shoes made of mountains"	November 11, 1979
67	Christmas: think of love, not presents	December 23, 1979
68	Marriner: a pearl before swine	May 9, 1980
69	A couch is his fire truck	July 28, 1980
71	Her commitment is infectious	October 27, 1980
72	A washed out bride on the creek	December 28, 1980
73	Nell has friends with guns and clubs	February 25, 1981
74	Richard Harris: "Camelot" is a dream	July 16, 1981
76	Kara: she never asks "Why me?"	August 19, 1981
77	At 87, he's still airborne	October 12, 1981
78	Ever tried to bash a rubber mouse?	August 12, 1984
79	Ethel is not run of the mill	October 13, 1985
80	Jeffrey: he knew he was special	January 12, 1986
82	Get rid of one bag of complications a day	February 9, 1986
83	Holly: a very special trouper	March 2, 1986
84	I shouldn't have put out the fire	March 6, 1986
85	Charlie gets all clear to die	April 5, 1986
86	Legal racing hurts illegal bookies	September 7, 1986
87	High Rise Joe: a blind man who sees a lot	August 2, 1987
88	Nicollet Hotel was a city palace	September 13, 1987
89	A marriage envied in heaven	October 4, 1987
91	A baby grandson who got help	April 10, 1988
92	J. F. Powers: betting on god to win	September 4, 1988
93	He was paid for his favorite hobby	November 27, 1988
95	Halsey: set Scott's pants on fire	June 11, 1989
96	She learned to be a friend of Jesus	April 8, 1990
99	Who needs him? I guess I do *Larry Batson*	March 30, 1982

Foreword

Chekov in shorthand—that's Robert T. Smith. The one about the aging prostitute, for example. It's bar-closing time on Hennepin. Enter the woman. She's well over fifty, too old to turn a trick, but she persists. We follow her for a block or two. She's scorned by the men she approaches. Insulted. She turns a corner and meets one of her colleagues in a tight satin dress. They exchange a few words. And there we leave her, heading off into the night. That's it. That's all he wrote. But Smith leaves *us* with an indelible portrait of a moment in this woman's life. And he mostly does it in sentences like this one. Short.

Or the one about the retarded child on the city bus. Or the one about the woman running a marathon at the age of 76. Or the one about the woman Smith knew when he was a kid. She was the mother of a friend of his, and she had this strange habit. She read books.

Smith, like Chekov, loves people. You can tell by the way he delves into their souls. People you never heard of. And in the process, he stirs up something in the reader's soul. Pity. Anger. Nostalgia. Love.

Not all the souls are anonymous. Here, too, are dozens of famous people Smith has met during his long career in newspaper work: Danny Kaye, Jack Benny, Presidents Kennedy and Johnson, J.F. Powers, Richard Harris, Lilli Palmer, and Bryan Smith. Bryan is Smith's little boy, and I'm only kidding—Bryan isn't actually famous. But there are enough columns here about Bryan to *make* him famous.

Whatever you do, don't skip the introduction. It's Robert T. Smith's memoir in a twelve-page nutshell and it's packed with newspaper stories. It's a riot. The one about Ed Gein, for example . . .

JON HASSLER

Introduction

I was a cub reporter working for *The Minneapolis Tribune*. There had been a fatal traffic accident on Highway 12 in St. Louis Park. I was assigned, with Photographer Russ Bull, to cover it.

We arrived at the scene late. The body had been removed and the authorities were gone.

"Lie down on the road," said Bull to me.

"Why?" I asked.

"Just do it," he said.

I just did it.

Bull opened the trunk of his car and took out a white sheet. He put it over me and took a photo.

I was on page one of the *Tribune* the next morning.

I recite this story to indicate how things were in journalism in the 1940s. The reporters and photographers were characters in the main. Few were college graduates, they drank a lot and were not above such tactics as Russ Bull and the sheet.

One photographer carried a child's shoe with him. If a kid was hurt or killed, he would place the shoe at the spot of the incident and shoot a picture of it.

One reporter covered the Minneapolis Aquatennial Parade from a bar across the street from the newspaper. He had the lineup of the parade and would interject things such as: "At Fifth and Nicollet, a little girl ran into the street and was barely missed by a float."

Newsmen were not against taking things for free. Drinks, lunches, whatever. Russ Bull was particularly adept at soliciting handouts. Once there was a potato festival in northwestern Minnesota. Bull learned that Cedric Adams, a local press and television personality, was getting $5,000 to M.C. the event.

Russ was assigned to photograph the festival. He arrived by car and looked up the festival's chairman.

"Now, sir, I hear you're paying Cedric Adams $5,000," said Russ. "Now, I'm going to take pictures here for a large Minneapolis newspaper and . . ."

The festival chairman broke in: "Now, don't you worry. We are going to take good care of you, too."

Russ was elated—until he returned to his car after taking his pictures. The back seat of the car was filled with potatoes.

It was a tradition for public relations people to give newsmen bottles of booze at Christmas time. A lot of them.

All that ended in 1952, when John Cowles, Sr., the big boss of the newspapers, decreed that there would be no more freebees.

A bit later, near Christmas time, Daryle Feldmeir, managing editor of the *Tribune*, gave a speech to a state meeting of public relations people. The place roared with laughter when Feldmeir said:

"Now, I want you all to know that we no longer can take bottles of liquor at Christmas time. So, I don't want to see any bottles of liquor on my doorstep—at 2936 Pierce St. NE."

My first job was with *The Minneapolis Times* on 4th St. I had been in the navy for four years during World War II. I was in the V-12 program, which involved going to college while in the navy and graduating and then being commissioned as an ensign.

My degree was in chemistry, but I always wanted to write and decided to become a newspaperman. I had already applied at *The Minneapolis Tribune,* but was told to go to some small town and get some experience.

I then approached the *Times*. I got an appointment with the managing editor, Manus McFadden, a crusty old guy. During the interview, he asked me if I was a journalism graduate. I got up and started for the door.

"Where you going?" asked McFadden.

"I didn't graduate from any journalism school." I replied.

"Good," said McFadden. "If there's anything I can't stand, it's journalism schools. You learn newspapering on the job."

So, I was hired. I learned later that

ROBERT T SMITH — Introduction

McFadden had not graduated from high school.

The *Times* was an old-time newspaper, majoring in police stories. It was owned by the Cowles family to give an appearance of competition in Minneapolis. It was an appearance only.

The city editor was, among other things, a racist. We identified every black when involved in stories. Then John Cowles, Sr., decreed that blacks were not to be identified unless pertinent to the story.

So, our city editor ordered photos taken of every black in a story. It took Cowles, Sr., about two months to catch up to that.

Our city editor also used me to get back at his experienced reporters. He would be unhappy with a story and yell: "Smith, come up here." Then he'd hand me the story and say: "See if you can make some sense of this."

All I did was dicker a bit with the lead. Then the city editor would loudly proclaim: "Well, that's more like it."

The first time that happened, I was devastated. But the experienced reporters told me not to worry. They knew the city editor's motives and didn't blame me.

The *Times* was folded about a year after I was hired. I was one of those, including Sid Hartman and Barbara Flanagan, who were transferred to *The Minneapolis Tribune.*

I covered just about every beat there was, including police. There was a police reporter for the St. Paul newspaper who was the laziest man available. But one day, it paid off.

There was a murder in the Minneapolis suburb of Fridley and we were on deadline. We all rushed out to cover it. The St. Paul reporter was taking one of his many naps.

When we got to the crime scene, the police already had left. And the body had been taken to the morgue. It was too late for us to get the story in.

But when we got back to our offices in City Hall, we learned the worst. The police had returned to their City Hall headquarters, had awakened the St. Paul reporter and gave him the story.

The news business leveled out in the mid-fifties. No more taking things for free, no more faking the news. It was strictly on the legitimate side.

I rose in rank, became an assistant city editor and then, in 1956, at age 30, city editor of the *Tribune*. At the time, I was the youngest city editor of a major newspaper in the nation. *Time* magazine did a piece on me for the Press section. During my tenure as city editor, the *Tribune* was named one of the 10 best newspapers in the United States three times.

A lot of that had to do with some specialists we had: Sam Romer, on labor; Victor Cohn, on medicine and science, and Carl Rowan, on race relations.

Carl, who went on to be a famous government official and national columnist, was the first black person we hired. He had a stormy beginning.

The first night he was there, we all took him out to dinner at a nearby bar-restaurant. Back in those days, there still was a lot of open discrimination against blacks.

The owner of the restaurant, seeing Carl, told us we were not welcome. We argued, but he was adamant.

We went elsewhere. That night the discriminatory bar-restaurant burned to the ground.

To this day, the owner thinks we did it.

Then there was the time I assigned Carl to cover a dinner at the swank Minneapolis Club. It was for a high State Department official.

Also attending was our executive editor, Bill Steven. He was more a promotion expert than an editor.

I got a call from him at the City Desk:

"What in hell are you doing" he yelled. "Sending that black to the Minneapolis Club."

"He's the most qualified," I said.

Steven huffed and puffed and then returned to the party.

He looked up and saw Carl sitting next to the high State Department official at the head table. Steven was amazed.

The official had met Carl and was most impressed with him. He invited him to be his head table guest.

12

Steven never complained about Carl again.

Another Steven story:

The Metropolitan Stadium was about to be built. It was to be financed largely by city bonds. Frank Wright was then covering City Hall and came in with a story pointing out that the bonds were not secured. There was some risk to the buyers.

I offered the story for page one at the news huddle. Steven was shocked:

"We can't run a story like that. It could kill the whole project."

I told him we were in the reporting business, not the stadium building business.

Steven ignored me, and killed the story.

Frank Wright resigned, the managing editor resigned and I resigned.

The next morning we all were called into the office of the big boss, Gideon Seymour. He asked me what it was all about. I told him.

He looked at Steven and said:

"Bill, what the hell are you doing. The story is not only legitimate, but we betray our readers by not running it. We are in the newspaper business, not the stadium promotion business."

He ordered the story on page one the next morning.

We all unresigned.

And then there was Paul Presbrey, a unique individual, a rare specimen. He lived reporting. He loved reporting. Nothing else was as important in his life. He also was a photographer.

Some Presbrey stories:

The Ed Gein story broke. He was the Wisconsin psycho who killed women and then had them for dinner.

When the story first unearthed, I sent Presbrey to cover it. He had many years of reporting and has seen just about everything.

Presbrey checked out the story, and then called me with the understatement of the century:

"You know, Smith, this borders on the bizarre."

Part of a building collapsed in downtown Minneapolis. A woman was trapped in the debris. She later called me and said she wanted to tell me her story:

"There I was, lying under a lot of heavy stuff. I didn't know what was going to happen next. I was really scared. Would more of the building fall on me?"

"And then I was him. A man was running toward me. 'Saved, at last,' I thought. 'Thank God!'"

She said the man stopped about 10 feet from her. He leveled a camera at her and took her picture. He then whirled and ran away.

Yeah, Presbrey!

A woman was murdered in St. Paul. Her body was found in an alley. Presbrey showed up, took one look at the body and said to the police:

"Hey, I know this woman. And I know who killed her. She was my father-in-law's mistress. He was having troubles with her."

Sure enough. Presbrey's wife's father did it.

Now, Presbrey's wife was terribly upset with him for turning her father in, resulting in her father going to prison. And she stayed angry.

When the killer first came up for parole, a mere formality. Presbrey called the parole board and told them he and his wife were coming to the parole board hearing.

"No matter what I say," said Presbrey. "don't pay any attention to it.

At the hearing, Presbrey gave a passionate pleas for the release of his father-in-law. He was really eloquent.

His wife was most pleased and finally forgave him.

And, yes, the parole board didn't pay any attention.

Presbrey decreed in his will that he would pay for a huge party for his friends to honor his death. Well, he died and the party was scheduled in a large St. Paul mansion.

We all attended. Free drinks, free food, free entertainment. Ah, well, not quite. Presbrey had done everything but provide the money for the party. We all chipped in.

By 1960, I was getting antsy. I wanted back on the street, reporting and writing

ROBERT T SMITH

again. I was tired of being tacked to a desk.

Some friends of mine at *Time* magazine heard of my situation. There was a desperate need for a News Editor of the Washington Bureau of *Time*. I didn't want it, but I was told if I could straighten out that bureau I could go any place in the world as a reporter.

Also, John Kennedy was running for president and I liked the idea of being in Washington if he were president. And I was pretty sure he would be.

I took the job. As it turned out, all the bureau needed was a City Editor. They had tried reporters in the job. They hated it and were lousy at it.

It took me about three months to get the bureau in order. By then, I had fallen in loved with Kennedy.

Things were different when Kennedy became president. We would sit around the White House swimming pool with the president. It was understood such sessions were off the record.

Kennedy told us how much he hated his wife, Jackie. And he told us of some of his exploits with other women. For instance, there were two beautiful blondes employed in the White House. We called them Fiddle and Faddle.

They couldn't type or take shorthand or do much of anything. Except take care of the president.

So, why didn't we report such things? Back then, there was a rule: personal things about the president were not reported unless they endangered the presidency or the life of the president.

That was demonstrated when Lyndon Johnson became president. We were down in Johnson City, Texas, one weekend. On Sunday morning, Johnson came out of his house with a beer in one hand and a blonde in the other. He jumped into his convertible and went speeding 80 miles an hour down the road.

He was endangering the life of the president. We all reported it. Johnson knew the rules and never complained about the stories.

All that changed, of course, with Richard Nixon. His handling of Watergate and other things made personal things about a president fair game. It became popular to try to be an exposer.

It has been that way ever since. Take President Clinton, for example. Many personal things about him have been revealed.

There are many memories of Washington. One time, two young high school students, a boy and a girl, were named winners of a Future Farmers of America competition. One of their rewards was a visit with President Kennedy.

I contacted the boy ahead of time and asked him to come back to me after the Kennedy meeting and tell me what happened. Might be a story for *Time*, I thought.

Well, the boy came back and reported:

"We entered the Oval Office and the president got up and shook my hand. And then he spent the rest of the time with the girl."

In Washington, my wife and kids were at the stop light when they were rear-ended by a 1956 Buick.

There was some damage to our car and I took it to two repair shops for estimates. The largest was $800.

The next day, the insurance representative of the guy who did the damage, came to our house. He didn't ask for the estimates. He said: "Would three thousand dollars solve everything?" Certainly.

He had me sign a waiver of any other action. Then, I asked him how come?

"Well," he said, "we checked out our client and discovered he insists that he is Teddy Roosevelt. The real Teddy Roosevelt.

"Now, if the thing went to court, we'd be exposed as the company who insured some nut who thinks he's Teddy Roosevelt. That wouldn't help our image at all. So, we decided to settle and quick."

Henry Luce, the co-founder of *Time* magazine, was a Republican of the first front. But he also was a man who wanted the truth, wanted facts.

Introduction ROBERT T SMITH

As editor of *Time*'s Washington Bureau, I had just hired a young fellow who had worked for the *New York Herald Tribune* in Paris.

Luce came down to Washington for a dinner with the members of the bureau. He began expounding on France, with some of his pet theories. The newcomer from Paris said:

"You're wrong, Mr. Luce."

Luce was a bit taken aback. But he quizzed the newcomer on the subjects and the newcomer was most-knowledgeable and concrete.

Luce was impressed. He didn't mind being wrong if you could convince him you were right.

After the meeting, members of the bureau were convinced the newcomer better find a new job. I wasn't worried.

Luce came up to me and took me aside: "Who is that new young man?" I told him. Said Luce: "He's a keeper."

A different Luce story:

The big boss, in 1964, wanted to know the chances of Barry Goldwater becoming president. Our bureau chief at the time decided to give Luce what he wanted to hear. Not what he should hear.

Our White House correspondent and I tried to talk him out of it. We told him Goldwater didn't have a chance, that Lyndon Johnson had the Kennedy legacy and nothing or no one could beat him.

But the bureau chief prevailed.

Of course, Goldwater was a disaster. Luce had acted on the bureau chief's information and was most embarrassed.

We got a new bureau chief.

Hedley Donovan, a Minnesota creation, was Luce's closest ally. And I was present at more than one meeting in New York when Donovan proved that.

The scenario went like this:

Luce would come up with a "great idea." He was one of those creative people who didn't know whether his ideas were any good. Sometimes they were and sometimes . . .

Well, Luce would outline his idea. The brown-nosers at the meeting, who were almost all of those there, would laud Luce for his genius. "Wonderful, Mr. Luce . . ." "Brilliant, Mr. Luce . . ."

And then it would come Donovan's turn:

"No," he would say. And that ended that.

Donovan didn't always say no. But Luce counted on him to weed out the bad ideas. Donovan later succeeded Luce as the head of *Time*.

My main memory of Kennedy occurred one night when I went to the movies with Orville Freeman, then Secretary of Agriculture. We sat in the balcony of a theater near the White House.

A voice behind us said: "How come you're not working, Orville?" It was Kennedy, who had sneaked out of the White House with his Secret Service people.

After the film, we went to a local restaurant that had a private room for the president. There was some small talk, then Kennedy said:

"Oh, I know I haven't done a lot in my first term. I didn't get much through Congress. But you wait for my second term. I'm going to fight for the poor, the blacks, the elderly, the sick.

"Oh, I know. My first term was lukewarm. I had to learn the ropes. I was new to the job and it showed. I did pretty well in the foreign field. Got some things done there. I know my first term was, at best, a C minus experience. But you wait for my second term."

That was one month before November 22, 1963.

On the day Kennedy was shot and killed, I was alone in London. It was night and I unpacked at the hotel, had a light supper and went to the theater to see a play.

After the play, I strolled the London streets and noticed a lot of bustle. There were newsies hawking "Extras" telling of Kennedy's assassination. I was stunned.

When I got back to my hotel, I had a drink at the bar and then went up to my room. I found a note stuck under my door. It read:

"Dear Mr. Smith:

"I know you are an American. I just

wanted to say how badly I feel for you. I know that Americans liked Mr. Kennedy a lot. And I know you will miss him very much.

"You are alone in a foreign country and that must be especially difficult at this time. Please accept my feelings of sorrow for you."

It was signed by the maid.

There was no trick in organizing the *Time* Washington Bureau. It was under control in about three months. And then it just ran smoothly.

Of course, the New York brass thought I was a genius. And I didn't argue with them. Back then, *Time* was its old self. The same as it was when it was founded in the 1920's.

You had the front of the book, including national and foreign news. And then the back of the book, with movies, theater, music and so on. Now, I don't know what *Time* is. It has lost its flavor, and turned in a series of long-winded stories. Sad.

After Kennedy was killed, I decided to call in my marker. They said I could go anywhere in the world and I chose Paris.

I went there to arrange things for my family—wife and four kids. There was a hotel about a block from *Time* and I decided to stay there.

The hotel clerk asked me how long I wanted to stay. I said three days.

"Three days!" said the clerk. "But, Monsieur, that is most unusual."

I asked the clerk how much the room cost.

He said $50 an hour. That would be $3,600 for three days.

Of course, it finally came to me that it was not your ordinary hotel. It was one of those places where you take a woman for a relatively short visit.

So, I thanked the clerk with an embarrassed smile and decided to look for another, more conventional hotel.

At this point in history, all stories in *Time* had a one line headline . . .

In Paris, I covered the funeral of Rubirosa, the famed national lover. A number of lovely young women also attended.

As they were lowering the casket at the cemetery, a young blonde leaned over and whispered: "Il etait toujours pret."

Now, for the non-French speakers, that means he was always ready. But in France, it refers to his sexual ability.

I dutifully put it in my file to New York. The writer there liked it and put it in the story.

But the managing editor got leery. He figured it was a bit risqué for *Time*'s readers. So, he edited it out.

What he failed to realize was the headline, not edited out, was: "Il etait toujours pret."

A young black man came into my Paris office one day. He was homeless and hungry. But he was a smart American and he had a writing background.

I was deputy bureau chief of Paris at the time. The young black wanted a job so he could eat.

I assigned him some research projects. He did them well and I kept him employed.

He later made a movie in France and wanted to submit it to the San Francisco Film Festival. But the French government unveiled its well-known red tape and the film couldn't reach San Francisco by the deadline.

The young black came to me. Could I somehow help?

I cabled Time's bureau chief in San Francisco. He contacted the Film Festival people. An extension in time was arranged.

And the young black's movie won a first prize.

A day before the young black was to return to America, he came to me to say goodbye.

"Smith," he said, "there's one thing I want you to know. If ever you need anything—I don't care what it is. Money. Influence. I mean anything. I want you to keep one thing in mind: I won't know you."

You gotta love a guy like that. In this case, the guy was Melvin Van Peebles, who went on to make well-respected and popular movies. His son, Mario, is a prominent movie actor.

Introduction   ROBERT T SMITH

Working in Paris was most difficult for an American. The pace of life in France is slow. Most French people are not going anywhere in their jobs, so why bother?

New York would contact us in the morning and demand a file on someone by that afternoon. The only answer was making contacts ahead of time.

We wined and dined hundreds of government officials and others in France. One of those we seduced was Peter Ustinov, the movie actor and director. He loved the lunches and we enjoyed his wit and charm.

One morning, I got a cable from New York. "We have a story on Gore Vidal and we desperately need an interview with Ustinov. He hates Vidal, and we know he hates dealing with the media. Seldom gives an interview. But do your damndest to get him to talk."

I had the complete interview with Ustinov by early afternoon. I got back a cable: "Wonderful! How on earth did you do it?"

I never told them about the lunches.

One of my favorite stories involves *Time*'s London Bureau. They were overwhelmed with work at one point. There was a story about a stripper having an affair with a member of the royalty. But they had no one to cover it.

I volunteered. I telephoned the stripper from Paris to make an appointment. It was difficult often for Europeans to understand magazine reporters.

So, I identified myself as a newspaperman.

The stripper laughed robustly. I had no idea why.

After the interview in London, I asked the stripper why she laughed when I told her I was a newspaperman.

"Well," she said, "I don't know about America, but in England a newspaperman is a guy who goes to a burlesque show, puts a newspaper over his lap and puts his hand under the newspaper."

Shortly after I arrived in Paris, I went to Longchamps, the famed horse race track. I bought a program and leafed through it.

It was in French, and my French wasn't yet that good. But the numbers were numbers.

In the third race, there was a horse who had been out 14 times, had won 12 times and had come in second twice. Won't pay peanuts, I figured. But I put a whole $20 on him.

As expected, the horse won easily. As not expected, it paid 30 to 1. I got $600.

I returned to the *Time* office in Paris and said to a French woman employee: "I'm going to quit and just bet on the races."

I told her the story. She asked for the racing program.

"You dummy," she said. "That horse hadn't run for 18 months. It had a bad accident, an injured leg. That race was considered as just a warmup, an entre to racing again. No one thought he would win."

If I had known that, I wouldn't have bet on him.

While on racing: I was at Hollywood Park one day and noticed, in one race, a horse named Isadore Finkelstein. I had cheered many a horse in the stretch but never an Isadore Finkelstein.

So, just so I could cheer that name, I bet on him. I thought it was throwing away money as Isadore was a 24 to 1 shot.

The horses came into the stretch. "C'mon Isadore Finkelstein," I yelled. The people around me seemed to think I had lost my mind.

Well, Isadore won, much to my surprise.

At that point, people around me wanted to know who I was going to bet on next.

Art Buchwald also was a friend of the *Time* bureau in Paris. He had been a columnist from Paris for *The New York Herald Tribune* for years.

Then he went to Washington, D.C., to start a nationally syndicated column. He came back to Paris for a visit and I threw him a fancy lunch at Maxim's.

Then, he went to London where the son of Henry Luce was bureau chief. The son had not inherited Henry's largesse.

Art went to the London bureau and confronted young Luce. "How about a lunch for me?" asked Art.

17

ROBERT T SMITH   Introduction

Young Luce said no.

Retorted Art: "Well, Smith in Paris gave me a great lunch at Maxim's."

Needless to say, I heard from New York about that. Thanks, Art.

One night I was driving from Paris to the west coast of France. I was alone. And then I had a flat tire.

I was up in the hills somewhere. The flat didn't thrill me, but I had no choice but to get out and fix it. No Highway Helpers in France.

Well, I'm glad I got out. It was a most unusual experience. The sky, I swear, was about 20 feet above me. And it was spectacular. A more beautiful scene I never have witnessed.

I just sat down and stared. The feeling was eerie. It was, as if, some magic had descended on me and me alone. There was no one near me. I must have spent an hour just staring at that fantastic sky—almost close enough to reach.

The Hollywood types were having a lunch aboard a Bateau Mouche, one of those boats that travel the Seine, mainly at night. They were promoting a new American movie that had just hit Paris.

I boarded the boat and took a window seat near the front. There were some pretty young women aboard and some stars of the movie.

Then, an older woman boarded. She wasn't beautiful and appeared to have been around the block, as the cliché goes, many times.

She looked around and then came and sat next to me. She smiled and the miles of wear seemed to disappear. Her talk was not centered on herself. She wanted to know about me.

Finally, she allowed some chatter about herself. She told me she loved to cook—especially mushrooms. She told me she adored the sea—any sea. "It calms me," she said. "And lord knows, I need to be calm."

For the whole trip, she had me mesmerized. She knew how to entertain in a modest setting. When the trip was over, I realized I didn't know her name.

As she was leaving, I apologized for not asking sooner for her name. She smiled and said softly: "Simone Signoret."

At one point, *Time* decided to do a cover on Norman Mailer. The magazine had not treated Mailer with much respect, but he was getting more famous every day.

Time wanted an interview with William Buckley, Jr., a longtime enemy of Mailer. He was in Gstaad, Switzerland, at the time. I made the trip.

I found Buckley in a ski lodge above Gstaad. It was lunch time and he invited me to eat with him.

"We can talk during lunch," he said.

But some hangers-on showed up and an interview was impossible. Buckley knew my concern and whispered that we would have dinner that night at his place. No interruptions. He would pick me up at my hotel.

I expected the rich man to arrive in a limousine. He came in a Volks bug. We had supper in his huge dining room—Buckley at one end of the table, his wife at the other and me in the middle.

Afterwards, we went into his study. He began:

"First of all, *Time* is not going to do a cover on Norman. They don't like him and, in its history, the only time that *Time* did a cover that was not upbeat was one on Hitler."

But he was very generous in terms of the interview. And he was a very good interviewee. It was mostly a matter of just taking notes.

I got back to Paris and cabled the interview. The next morning, I got a cable from New York:

"Wonderful interview of Buckley. Good job."

The next morning, I got another cable from New York:

"We have decided not to do a cover on Mailer."

One theory I developed in life is that beauty is boring. The initial beckoning of beauty is fascinating. You see a beautiful woman, in the American sense. The model type.

Introduction

ROBERT T SMITH

Everything about her is average. Average nose, average chin, average height, average whatever. So, after she's around for a while, she, in looks terms, gets boring.

I got another slant on that in the Swiss mountains while on the Buckley assignment. I got into Gstaad late at night and went right to bed.

I awoke the next morning, pulled the curtain on the picture window in my room and, voila!, the most beautiful scenery I had ever witnessed.

The mountains shone in the sun, with patches of green and patches of snow. It was awesome.

The next morning I pulled the curtain. OK, a nice scene. By the fourth day, I didn't even pull the curtain.

The east side of Paris has some pretty lousy neighborhoods. A lot of street crime. A lot of kids running loose.

I was covering a story in one of those neighborhoods when I ran across a girl. She was Nicole, and she was 10. She couldn't read or write and hadn't been in school in years.

A while later, I was going to Versailles, the home of Louis XIV's huge castle. I got an idea: why not take Nicole and give her a bit of experience away from the street?

That I did. Nicole had never been out of east Paris. She loved the French countryside and, especially, she loved the castle. She stared at the wall paintings in the castle—and the statues. She wandered the lush gardens outside.

And then I took her home.

I got to thinking: what a big shot you are? I said to myself. You expose a little girl to culture and then you dump her back into poverty and degradation. Aren't you something, I said. Big deal.

For a long time, I felt terrible about that. But then, about two years later, I got a note from Nicole. That in itself was startling. When I last saw her, she couldn't write. The note said:

"Dear Monsieur Smith:

"I want to tell you about my life. I have been in school for two years now and I can read and write. Not great yet, but I'm trying. Also, I have quit the streets—I'm living with my grandparents in a nice house.

"It all started with the trip to Versailles. I saw, for the first time, that there was something more than the streets. I saw beautiful flowers and paintings. I am planning to stay in school and try to make something of myself. Thank you for that trip."

Aboard the SS France en route from France to the United States:

I had gotten to know James Jones, author of *From Here to Eternity* and many other novels. By coincidence, he and his wife were aboard the France, as was my family.

We got together for dinner one night. I was sitting next to Jimmy's wife, a large, but in no way fat, woman.

A drunk at the next table started in on Jimmy.

"So, you think you're some hotshot writer, do you?" the drunk said. "Well, I say, you're lousy."

The drunk, with similar jibes, kept at it. Jimmy, a rather small man, was getting upset.

Jimmy's wife leaned over to me and said:

"You know what's going to happen? That drunk is going to keep going and then Jimmy is going to get really angry and then . . .

"I'm going to have to go over and deck the bastard . . .

Another Jones tale:

Jimmy was a prolific drinker. And sometimes he and his wife would get squabbling. They lived in an apartment overlooking the Seine.

One night they were going at it strong, screaming and all. Jimmy ripped off his wedding ring, threw open a window and tossed the ring into the river.

His wife told me the rest:

"I woke up the next morning and Jimmy was gone. That was not unusual. I puttered around a little and then went to the window to look at the Seine.

"I looked down and there was Jimmy diving into the river. He was looking for his ring."

ROBERT T SMITH   Introduction

Jim Wilde was unique. He was a correspondent in the Paris office of *Time*. He was a good reporter, an excellent writer and, of course, he was crazy.

Wilde had no time for discipline. Making out his expense accounts didn't interest him. In those days, we drew money for expenses and then accounted for it.

I was deputy bureau chief of *Time* and, thus, was responsible for reporters doing such book work. They cabled me that Wilde was way behind and he had better get the reports in. Or else.

Wilde shrugged and walked away. The next day, he asked if he could go to Algeria (We covered French-speaking Africa).

He said it was time to research the region for possible stories—something we did fairly regularly. Things were quiet, so I said yes.

The next thing, I got a cable from New York. It included a message from Wilde in Algiers:

"I was out in my tent in the desert, doing my expense accounts. I had my typewriter on a stool and all my receipts.

"Suddenly, I was surrounded by radical Arabs. They were in a terrible mood. They began firing at my tent. I raced outside and hid in an oasis.

"Then, they set fire to my tent. Everything was destroyed, including the receipts. Sorry."

New York didn't believe it for a moment. But they were amused and excused Wilde in terms of his expense accounts.

While on Wilde:

We all were at a party in Paris one night. It was one of those snooty affairs with folks using big words and making boring statements.

In the midst of it all, Wilde stood up in the middle of the room and said:

"Masturbation is the only answer. It's cleaner and you meet a nicer set of people."

With that, Wilde left the party.

The Paris Bureau of *Time* covered North Africa, the Low Countries of Belgium, the Netherlands and Luxembourg, and Switzerland. I got to visit all these countries in my five years in France.

But my tenure in Paris was about to come to an end. *Time* was like the army. Four or five years in one place, and then on to another location. My next location was to be New York.

I hated New York as a father of four. As a single man, I could see its advantages. But not for me.

My mother, back in Minneapolis, became quite ill and I went to see her. While in Minneapolis, I visited the newspapers. I told the executive editor of *The Minneapolis Tribune*, Bower Hawthorne, about my unhappiness about New York.

"Ever thought of being a columnist?" he asked.

No, I hadn't. But he offered me the job and I took it.

After all, how difficult could it be to write a column? I found out quickly.

Art Buchwald talked to me about writing a column and gave me good insight:

"If they give you time, you will be all right. But, if they discover that after two months you don't have the highest readership and fire you, then . . ."

Well, the *Tribune* gave me time. And I lasted from 1968 to 1989, 21 years. It was the hardest job I ever undertook.

I remember the vacation gambit of the *Tribune*. When a regular columnist was on vacation, other staff members would fill in for him. They all had a wonderful idea for a column. Or maybe two or three ideas.

But they all discovered that they had to have more ideas. And that cured most of them from wanting to be a columnist.

About the vacation bit: the best sting on me was committed while I once was away having fun . . .

There was a guy at the *Tribune* I hated. He was a real jerk and had done everything he could to undermine me. He was one staffer selected to fill in for me while I was vacationing.

He wrote a column about conscientious objectors. About three days after I got back, I got a letter from a woman in Dallas, Texas. She wrote:

"I am a former Minneapolis resident and I have always loved your column. I

| Introduction | ROBERT T SMITH |

now take the *Tribune* by mail. And I want you to know that the best column you ever wrote was the one on conscientious objectors."

I went to The Little Wagon, a bar-restaurant hangout for *Tribune* people. And I complained bitterly about the letter. Among those at the Wagon was Dave Wood, the *Tribune* Book Editor.

"Gee, that's too bad, Smith," he said.

A day or so later, I got a letter from a man in San Diego, Calif. It was the same. He was a former resident of Mankato, Minn., and loved my column. But my best was the one on conscientious objectors.

Again, I went to the Wagon to cry.

Well, I got eight such letters from all over the United States. And one from Canada. They all basically loved the column on conscientious objectors.

Finally, Dave Wood confessed. He had been in the airport in St. Louis, Mo., and had a long wait for his plane. So, he wrote the letters—right handed, left handed, with a scrawl, with a shaky hand, whatever. Then he had given them to people in the airport who were going in all sorts of directions. He told them to mail the letter when they got home.

The story of my columning is in this book. So, enough said. But I would like to reveal a letter I got that I found fascinating.

The letter came from a woman in Bemidji, Minn. She wrote:

"I really love your column. You have such insight on human nature, and have a wonderful way of writing about it. . . ."

Then she listed four recent columns she particularly loved—and three of them were Jim Klobuchar's.

One compensation in column writing is what I call "Results Columns." I didn't write the columns just to get results. I wrote them because I thought they were good.

One of them was on Josie Colvin. She was 18-months-old and came to Minneapolis from the hills of Virginia. She had a problem: She had only half the normal amount of large bowel and only a tenth of the normal amount of small bowel. A very rare birth defect.

She had another problem: her parents were poor and had no insurance. Her conditions couldn't be corrected in Virginia, so she was sent to University of Minnesota Hospitals.

Josie needed a month's care at University hospitals. But, being from out-of-state, that month had to be paid for: a total of $9,000.

"If she doesn't get that month, she won't make it," said Dr. Harvey Sharp.

I wrote about Josie, and there was a photo with the column. It was the only coverage on the little girl.

The result: $47,000 came in. And not from rich folks. Most contributions were $1 to $20. The largest was $750.

Sven and Blanche Rydholm had been married 47 years. Sven, born in Sweden, was 74. As a last hurrah, he wanted to take Blanche to show her where he was born.

But there was no money for it. Sven had had heavy medical expenses. Blanche called me.

The result: hundreds of people responded. A total of $1,300 was contributed—more than enough for the trip at that time.

Karie Martin, 10, found a $100 bill on the floor of a shoe store. She reported the find to the store management.

Karie wanted that money to buy a new bicycle. It had been her dream for a long time.

But a "rich woman" claimed the money. No bicycle.

I heard about it and did a column on it.

The result: $200 for a new bike.

Mary Johnson, 75, lived on $200 a month Social Security and had $10 a month in food stamps.

She had saved $200 to buy Christmas presents for her grandchildren. A youth stole it from her.

The police, saddened by the theft, came to me.

ROBERT T SMITH

Introduction

The result: contributions totaling $1,200.

Those are some of the "Results Columns" involving me.

Journalism changed markedly during my career. It started out as a rather flamboyant affair. Police stories were prominent. Stories about education were practically non-existent.

Local news was in, national and foreign news barely tolerated.

Then things settled down. Journalism became more serious, more respectable. National and foreign news became much more important. Honesty became a must.

More and more reporters came out of college journalism schools. That was not a plus. A reporter needs to be a well-rounded, well-informed person. Not just someone who knows a bit about reporting and writing.

A rather common situation: I would hire a journalism school graduate and a graduate of a more rounded major. The journalism graduate would do better for about six months. The other major would be learning journalism during that time. Then, the other major would blossom and the journalism grad would be in status quo.

In conclusion, when it comes to humor, this little tale should fit. It involves a letter I once received. There was another Robert Smith with the Cowles newspapers. He was publisher of *The Minneapolis Star*. He died at a rather young age.

About two weeks later, I got a letter from a woman in Mankato, Minn. It was addressed correctly to me. She wrote:

"I'm sorry to hear you died . . ."

Then came her second line:

"Does this mean you won't be doing your column anymore?"

Robert T. Smith

ROBERT T. SMITH

COLUMNS 1968–1989

November 22, 1968   ROBERT T SMITH

Wait for my second term . . .

Nov. 22, 1963—Present John F. Kennedy was shot and killed today . . .

I knew Kennedy some. Not because of me, but because when he was president I was news editor of the Washington bureau of *Time* magazine. And Kennedy considered *Time* a valuable political outlet.

Whatever else he was, Jack Kennedy was a man of presence. He was one of those rare souls who dominated whatever space he was in.

I remember being in a room at the State Department one afternoon. It was a cocktail party for a minor official who was retiring.

There was no expectation that the president would arrive. I was talking to a woman with my back to the door when I suddenly said: "Kennedy is here."

I had not seen him, nor had she. But he had just entered the room.

It will be very surprising to me if he goes down in history as a great president. He was too worried about what the majority of Americans thought and not enough about forming that thought.

He was a charmer, but more a follower than a leader. He was late on civil rights, because that's what the majority wanted at the time. He was too much into Vietnam, because it was popular at the time.

We too often forget how wrong the majority can be. Mostly, the majority gets on the right track long after the damage is done. Vietnam. Nixon. Civil rights.

I remember one incident vividly, an event I have spoken about but never written about.

One night I went to the movies at a theater about two blocks from the White House. I was with a government official from Minnesota.

We sat in the balcony and, after about ten minutes, this Boston accent behind us asked the official, in a kidding way, why he wasn't working.

Kennedy had sneaked out of the White House, with his ever-present secret servicemen, to see the movie.

After it was over, we went to a Washington restaurant that had a private back room for presidential use.

For an hour Kennedy talked, chatted is probably a more apt word.

"Oh, I know, I haven't done much this first term, but you wait for my second term," he said.

He said he had gotten very little through Congress and had made a bit of a splash in Europe, but basically he had accomplished very little.

He had bungled at the Bay of Pigs, and was upset about getting more involved in Vietnam. But he was worried about re-election.

"In my second term, I am going to use all of the powers of the presidency and whatever I might have personally to help the people of this country," he said. "The poor, the handicapped, those discriminated against.

"And then, after my two terms, I plan to devote the rest of my life to those people. I was born rich. I don't have to worry about money. But I do have to worry about making some mark in the world."

Kennedy was intense. It was obvious that he was hurting. Not just his bad back, but his psyche, his emotional setup. He loved the idea of being president, but he had learned the tough way that it was a terrible responsibility.

Mainly he learned that, he said, during the Cuban missile crisis, where he had to

ROBERT T SMITH January 8, 1969

stare down the Russian leadership with Third World War as a possible consequence.

"Oh, I know, I know, I haven't done much this first term, but you wait for my second term," he repeated.

That was one month before Nov. 22, 1963 . . .

January 8, 1969

A touch of white stuff in New York

Late at night New York can be a lonely place . . . It's a good time to browse.

I had spent most of the daytime sitting in taxi cabs. A wee bit of snow had fallen and New York reacted like an elephant who had spied a mouse.

Traffic in this city of eight million is enough to contend with normally. But add a touch of the white stuff and the natives panic.

Why every New York taxi driver figures you're a rube I don't know. But twice, before I could scream, the cab I was in turned crosstown so that Times Square could be traversed.

It only takes one visit to New York before you know that crosstown is to be avoided if at all possible, and Times Square is a dirty word.

"Where are you going?" I asked the first driver.

"Times Square," he said.

"Why" I asked.

"I thought you'd like to see it. It's very famous."

"I was born there," I lied.

He grumbled and turned uptown. But even the usual uptown-downtown flow was stopped. People got out of cars in the middle of the street to chat.

What this town needed, I thought, was the efficient snow removal system of Minneapolis.

When I finally got to my hotel, I hid in my room until it was safe to come out—late at night. Then it was rather pleasant. The eight million apparently were all snug in their beds.

At midnight, I went to Grand Central. I had never been there except when thousands of commuters gathered.

Now it was nearly empty. Only then do you realize the size of the huge, old palace. It was the first time I'd noticed the painting on the block-high ceiling.

Just then two drunks, arm in arm, came by. One of them stopped short and pointed upward.

"Who's that up there?" he asked, pointing to a winged god on the ceiling carrying a club.

"Lindsay," said the other. They laughed and staggered out.

The Investment Information Center was closed. Only in New York would you have such a service in a depot. No wonder the ulcer rate is high.

The lower level was vacant, except for three Negro boys playing marbles. They couldn't have been more than 10. I wondered what was home for them.

"That's my steelie," said one.

"I was just looking at it," said another.

Then the only sound was the clicking of marbles.

On the upper level, some Ivy Leaguers were saying goodbye to their girlfriends.

"See you next Friday," said one.

"Be on time," said a small blonde with an imitation leopard coat.

A weary old train came in on track 13, deep in the innards of the station. Bare bulbs lighted the way up for the few passengers who solemnly left the New Haven "express."

Back on the upper level the sweepers were at work. New York's labor problems, this time with the railroad workers, was apparent from signs on the walls: "Vote for early retirement," "A new pension plan now."

I decided to walk up Fifth Av. in the night air. It was about 20, almost a spring day for a Minnesotan.

A man and woman, bundled to the chins, marched ahead of me.

"Have you ever seen such snow?" she said.

If I could have found enough to make a snowball I would have thrown it at them.

April 28, 1970   ROBERT T SMITH

Stripper Gypsy is a knitter

I spent an afternoon in Paris with Gypsy Rose Lee. She's dead now, and it's her wit I will miss.

In a way, it was an accident I met her that day two years ago. But a pleasant one.

I was working for *Time* magazine and was assigned to do a story on Janet Flanner, who has written "A Letter From Paris" for *The New Yorker* since that magazine was born.

Janet, who writes under the pen name Genet, lives in the elegant Hotel Continental on the Rue de Rivoli, across from the Tuileries gardens.

"Gypsy's here," she said. "Come and meet her."

I didn't attach the name to the famed stripteaser. We entered the hotel bar and made for a woman sitting in a corner knitting.

She Knitted a House

It was a huge thing that flowed over her back and onto the floor.

"What's that you're knitting?" I asked.

"A house," she said.

Gypsy and Janet had been friends for years. They talked of the oldtimers of *The New Yorker*—Thurber, Woollcott, Ross, Dorothy Parker.

Gypsy had known them, too. I was impressed with her command of the language, and her quickness with a clever phrase.

She talked of being offered a job singing, and I remembered her quip: "I'll sing in whatever key you want—like a drum."

We moved out of the Continental to a small restaurant on the Left Bank. Gypsy ordered enough food for a water buffalo.

"What about the figure?" I asked.

"I have an irrational fear of becoming Twiggy," she said.

She Was Grateful to Burlesque

Gypsy told of starting in show business at 5, of coming to Minneapolis in an act with her sister, June Havoc. She told of graduating from a Hopkins grade school.

She said she was glad burlesque died out, but was grateful it had made her rich. I remember her blaming the decline of burlesque on slum clearance.

Janet has lived in Paris since the early 1920s and knew the likes of Fitzgerald and Hemingway, whom she disconcertingly called "Ernie."

Gypsy seemed fascinated by the anecdotes of those literary expatriots, particularly their ability to consume huge quantities of liquor.

The subject of husbands came up. Janet never had one, and Gypsy had three. The old strip queen said she was through marrying.

I thought of a line she had used earlier: "No career woman should have more than three husbands."

The conversation turned to her wealth, acquired as a novelist, playwright and actress, as well as a stripper.

She was well known for her ability to take a dollar and make it into two.

Gypsy paused a moment and then delivered one of her patented lines that I'd enjoyed before:

"Husbands come and go, but annuities will last as long as I do."

No one wants her anymore

A street scene in Minneapolis:

It was about 1 o'clock on Sunday morning. The bars were releasing their clients onto Hennepin Av. It was chilly.

I first saw her as she walked a little too deliberately along the sidewalk. She had been drinking but she didn't seem to be drunk.

"Hi there, fella," she said to a man about 30 who came out of Mousey's Bar near 11th St. "You want to take me home?"

"No thanks, Grandma," he said, and he laughed. Two men with him joined in the laughter.

The expression on her face didn't change. She continued down Hennepin, her step slowing a bit.

It was hard to determine her age. She looked 60 but I suspect she was closer to 50.

She wore one of those phony satin dresses, cut too low and too high for her thin figure. She had thrown her tattered coat around her shoulders.

Her blond wig was cheap and in disarray. She had no hat and her shoes were not for walking.

"Hello, champ," she said to a man who had turned onto Hennepin off 9th St. "You lonely?"

"Not that lonely," he said and stepped up his pace to avoid her.

"Well, you're no Christmas tree ornament yourself," she said.

Three Men Didn't Even Look

The wind stirred a little and she put her arms into her coat. But she left it unbuttoned. Three men who came out of The Poodle near 8th St. didn't even look at her.

She stopped to stare in the window of Music City. Using it as a mirror, she tried to straighten her hair and smooth her dress.

"I'm not so bad," she said in a mumbling tone. Then she shrugged as if she didn't believe what she just said.

A policeman was coming toward her. He was about a half block away. She crossed Hennepin and started down the other side.

A younger woman, also alone, approached. She carried a parasol but it wasn't raining.

"How's it going, Brennie?" the younger woman asked.

"There've been better nights, Angie," said the older woman. "Your show go all right?"

"The same music, the same men, the same dance," said Angie. "Maybe things will pick up for you, Brennie."

"They'd better," said the older woman. Angie walked off.

Nice Features, But Her Eyes Are Dead

Brennie continued her route. By this time she was near 5th St. She stopped under a street light.

Her face was pale and she had not painted it. She had good features but her skin was rough in spots. Her eyes were dead.

A shabby drunk came lurching along. He was changing directions like a man caught in a House of Mirrors.

"Hey, Brennie, old pal," he said. "I need some soup."

"So do I," she said and continued walking.

I thought of the stories I'd read recently about the plight of the hookers, of how there are just too many amateurs nowadays with the pill and all.

And, even in the good times, a woman as old as Brennie was in trouble.

Two young college-types came out of The Saddle. Brennie saw them and, in a tired way, approached.

"Hi, boys, you looking for some action?" she asked.

The two young men were embarrassed. They did nothing, just hurried on. Then after a little distance, one said to the other: "What was that nightmare?"

Brennie buttoned her coat, shrugged and began walking a bit faster. I figured she had given up.

I watched her until she started across the bridge toward Nicollet Island.

January 9, 1972   ROBERT T SMITH

Berryman: Indifference never came

The violent winds in my gardens front & back have driven away my birds.
"His Toy, His Dream, His Rest,"
by John Berryman

It was as if cruelty and violence loved to tease him. He hated them, but he didn't know how to protect himself.

And so Friday morning, John Berryman, poet, scholar, teacher and very sensitive human being, leaped to his death from the Washington Av. bridge.

He had tried to go away Wednesday night. He wrote his wife, Kate, a note. "I am a nuisance," it said. He got as far as a bus stop, then came back.

On Friday morning, he told Kate he was going to his office at the University of Minnesota. "It's time I cleaned things up," he said. This time he didn't come back.

It is difficult to describe Berryman. Saul Bellow will tell you he was a great storyteller. Mark Van Doren will say he was a listener. His friend, Dr. A. Boyd Thomes, found him a gay, witty and sometimes hilarious man. His wife knew him as gentle and very quiet. I knew him a little, and I feel that everything anybody says about him is true.

Perhaps the main theme of his poetry is death. He brooded about it a great deal. But he would write delightful little poems for children, such as the following unpublished bit for the Thomes's daughters:

Peachy & Katherine, those are the daughters,
frisky as brooms,
swung on the swing and woofed in the rooms . . .
The whole world should be filled
with little girls.

Even poetry itself intimidated John. He started writing it at 19. "I developed a hatred for poetry which did me very well for years. But at last the hatred wore out."

Berryman wrote most of his poetry in the "Shakespeare room" at his home. "He always wanted to be helpful around the house, but never knew how he could be," said his wife.

The poet would sit by his desk and brood for hours, perhaps days, over a poem. He lost all sense of day or night. Then, often, he would write extremely rapidly. And no matter what the hour, he would call his friends all over the United States and read them his latest creation. "Then an awful thing happens," he once said. "I lose all interest in the poem. I figure it's no good. And I stamp up and down because I can't any more use it as a weapon against gentility."

Only a few people are poets to the bone. But Berryman was. It cost him a life of recurring depression. "Everything affected him so deeply, so strongly," said his wife. "War. Hate. Poverty. Discrimination. Unkindness . . ."

A few nights before his death, he made the following entry in his diary: "Wept at TV film about woman's fatal brain disease . . ."

Berryman, who often said he was a scholar masquerading as a poet, won the Pulitzer Prize for poetry in 1965 for *77 Dream Songs*. The *New York Times* called him "a superb and difficult poet who belongs in the absolute first rank of American poets."

Oklahoma-born, Berryman, as a youth, was an athlete, played baseball and ran the 200-yard dash. He often was seen last summer swimming in the Sheraton-Ritz

ROBERT T SMITH   April 10, 1972

Hotel pool. "Don't tell anybody you saw me in such an establishment place," he would say in jest. Perhaps one of his pressures was that he insisted on living in the immediate present. "He was monumentally overwhelmed with the concern for the moment," said a friend.

He was deeply affected by his father's suicide. "My father killed himself when I was 11, and I've never been the same since." he said. "I have a funny feeling that a father's death is the most important fact in a life. At last the cover is removed . . ." In one of his "Songs" he wrote:

*The marker slants, flowerless, day's
   almost done,
I stand above my father's grave with
   rage . . .
When will indifference come . . .*

For John Berryman, whose birds were driven away by violent winds, indifference never came.

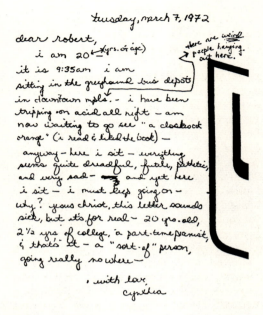

April 10, 1972

Someone going really nowhere

She tore a chunk of paper from a small white sack. She made an envelope out of what was left.

Then she wrote a letter to a stranger. Me. She signed only her first name, no address or other identifying bits.

It's not a new story these days: a confused, hurt, desperate young woman whose bridge to security has collapsed.

She gives no details of the incidents in her life that led her to sit alone that morning in a bus depot. She wasn't leaving town. Just waiting until a movie theater opened. So she could go there and sit alone.

There are avenues of help for her, if she's ready. If she wants to contact me, I'll tell her where she might go. Confidentially, of course. The letter tells the rest:

March 10, 1974

Butterflies are chasing her now

To love something, sometimes you have to free it.   **The Sandpiper**

Cecily took off at top speed. She swept across the fields, occasionally dodging nothing. She ran until she was exhausted, then she collapsed under a tree.

Cecily is free now. Out of her prison. She's in the country near White Bear Lake, with 10 whole acres of land to sniff and explore. Now she can run anytime.

We had Cecily, part Labrador and part something else, almost two years. It was our fault to begin with. We were attending a function at the Animal Humane Society of Hennepin County. Wife Janet noticed this golden puppy.

We did not know at first that Cecily had, as Yeats put it, "the will of the wild birds." We didn't know that rooted in her was a compulsion to be free of barriers of any sort.

We might have guessed when, as a puppy, she would often deliberately run into a wall, as if she could tumble it down and get at the world.

Then there were our futile attempts to

March 28, 1974 ROBERT T SMITH

keep her in an outside pen. They went on for well over a year, and included fencing and chicken wire and 10-foot sheets of plywood.

Cecily would work at some vulnerable spot in the enclosure until she got out. At one point, she learned how to open the gate. Several times she cut herself diving through small openings she had torn in the fence.

And, when we finally made the prison unconquerable, she began to bark all day. We decided she would have to be a house dog. She decided she wasn't one. She didn't bark inside, but it was apparent she yearned to be out.

If we were not careful in opening doors, she would be gone in a streak of gold. Last spring, she escaped and was bounding free between Lake Calhoun and Lake of the Isles. She was hit by a car, dragged 40 feet. Her right rear leg was injured.

I wrote about it at the time and received mail from people who said we were remiss in not keeping Cecily somehow tied up. I would guess none of those people ever had an Olympic pole vaulter for a dog.

When not escaping, Cecily would sit on the enclosed front porch and stare at the world she wanted to get at. It became more and more apparent she was unhappy in her comfortable prison.

Cecily was mainly Janet's dog. It was Janet who played with her and talked to her and fussed over her and loved her much. Although not happy enclosed, Cecily adored Janet. If Janet were within two blocks of the place, Cecily knew it.

It was Janet who had the tough decision. She kept asking me if I thought Cecily would be happier in the country. She knew the answer. I said yes, but that it would have to be her decision, since Cecily was mainly her dog.

Janet talked about freeing things you love. It doesn't only apply to animals. They came Friday and took Cecily to the country. Janet earlier had privately released her feelings.

As Cecily left, Janet said, "I'll just keep thinking of her chasing butterflies—and butterflies chasing her."

March 28, 1974

A picturesque divorce . . .

This comes under the heading of Well-Now-We've-Heard-Everything. It's common to have a photographer take pictures at your wedding. But your divorce?

A friend and neighbor, Robert H. White, of 3033 Knox Av. S., works for the post office, but is an excellent wedding photographer on the side. Four years ago, he did the wedding of a couple who were very pleased with his work.

The suburban couple, John, 32, and Mary, 29, didn't make a success of their marriage and decided to end it. There were no children involved and neither one blamed the other for the failure of the marriage. Both parties tend toward a bizarre sense of humor. One night, in jest, Mary said: "Why don't we have our divorce photographed—like our wedding?" John laughed and said: "Why not?"

Another martini or two, and the decision was made. White figured his task was not to reason why, but to take pictures. And the enterprise began.

The first picture was a marriage license burning ceremony. The couple stood around a silver bowl and touched long-stemmed matches to the document.

Mary and John were wed in a civil ceremony before a judge. For their divorce picture, they took back their rings. How can you tell if they are taking the rings back or giving them? "You really can't," said White, "but they know."

Then, of course, there was the divorce reception. The couple invited the people who attended the wedding. Everyone was asked to wear dark clothes. Instead of a cake-cutting scene, there was a picture of John and Mary standing by a cake platter with nothing on it.

Mary then threw a "divorce bouquet" to one of her friends who is having trouble with her marriage. The words "Just Divorced" were painted on the couple's two cars.

"It was all done in good spirit," reports

White. "For a while, I forgot it wasn't a wedding. Everyone seemed so cheerful."

John and Mary (not their real names) don't figure they have started a trend. "It's just that divorce in so many cases is filled with such anger and accusation," said Mary. "We wanted people to know that, although we failed, we weren't running around telling horrible stories about each other. Divorce can be a beginning, not an end."

John agreed: "We still respect each other. It just was a situation that wasn't working and was better ended."

White had to make two sets of prints for the black-bound divorce albums.

As a finale, John carried Mary over the threshhold, out of the house. Then they got into their separate cars and drove away.

November 17, 1974

A visit by hypocrisy

A street scene in Minneapolis . . .

It was a chilly night and Randy Siems, 20, was hitchhiking near 26th St. and Hennepin Av. He wasn't having too much success.

Randy had been visiting his nephew in south Minneapolis and was returning home to 4250 Humboldt Av. N. He is a college drop-out and has been trying to find work. Not much success there either.

A man came out of a nearby building and watched Randy trying to thumb a ride. He approached Randy and said: "Hitchhiking doesn't seem too good."

"No," said Randy, "seems like people don't want to pick me up."

Then the man said: "If you die tonight will you go to heaven? Can I show you how you can be sure?"

The man, one of the Jesus People, wanted a few minutes to talk to Randy about Jesus. "I gave up on organized religion," said Randy. "I found it hypocritical. I've been trying to find God by myself."

Randy said he knew some Jesus People who he thought had the right idea—to help people, to practice the original Christianity. So, he stepped back on the curb and listened to the man.

"If you can let Jesus into your heart your troubles will be over," said the man. "That's what I did and I have been reborn."

They talked for about 15 minutes and Randy told the man of his struggle for identity. He told him that doing things for your fellow-man was important, more important in Randy's mind than piety.

It was getting late and the cars were few.

They discussed hypocrisy. "People say they believe in God and then they do opposite things," said Randy. "What happens to love your neighbor and try to help him?" Randy told the man he once considered the ministry and had taught Sunday School for a year.

The man said the way to get your sins forgiven was to accept the Holy Ghost. Randy was impressed and, as they parted, he said: "Have a nice night."

Randy went back to hitch-hiking. In a few minutes, the man he had been speaking to approached in his car.

He waved at Randy and drove on by.

December 29, 1974   ROBERT T SMITH

Jack Benny: a terrible beginner

There was this young violinist who was quite average. And then he became a comedian and was a flop for quite a while. But when Jack Benny died at 80 he was one of the top entertainers in the world.

Will today's younger stars, any of them, be at the top when they get old? Will Paul Newman or Robert Redford or, God forbid, Burt Reynolds, outlast their good looks and sex appeal? Maybe Benny himself answered it.

I met Benny in New York when I was with *Time* magazine. It was an interview on the subject of longevity in entertainment. Benny was appearing at the Waldorf-Astoria Hotel.

Benny was easy to talk with, made no attempt to be funny or cute and, if modesty is truth, he had it. The great comedian said he was a terrible beginner. That was in 1912 and he did small bits in vaudeville that drew gales of silence most of the time.

"If I had started 20 years later, I don't think I could have even gotten a job as a theater doorman," said Benny. "Thirty years later, I know I wouldn't have made it."

But in 1912, vaudeville was in most cities of any size and there was room for all levels of talent.

"I can remember when 'Why-does-a-chicken-cross-the-road?' was one of the better jokes I stole," said Benny. "You learn a lot about humility and about people when you get booed off the stage. Either you quit, and in those days starve, or you try to get those people on your side."

The gentle man lit a cigar and said he was born without any natural talent: "They talk about my great sense of timing. That took years. Maybe decades. Can you imagine The Pause during vaudeville days. They would have strung me up with the curtain rope."

The comedian said he tried everything from a drunk act to a sophisticated Romeo role. All were disasters. Then he tried being the butt of the jokes. People began to laugh and never stopped.

Benny also surrounded himself with talent that fed that image. "Sometimes people forget that many of the laughs were lines from Dennis Day or Phil Harris or Mary Livingstone or Sheldon Leonard."

Will today's stars last through the years? "It's possible, but I doubt it," said the comedian. "They burn them out too quickly. Television. Movies."

He said it takes a long time for people to identify with an entertainer. He said people laugh at many things because they know so much about a long-standing entertainer. And it's important to span generations. "People who first liked me got their children to listen," he said. "Then those children got their children interested. Then you have a child, his parents and his grandparents all on your side."

In today's entertainment world, with its massive outlets, the child, his parents and grandparents are apt to have separate heroes. Except for the present oldtimers such as Bob Hope and, until Friday, Jack Benny.

ROBERT T SMITH   January 2, 1975

He relied on imagination and humor

John Irvin Hines Jr., 71, is gone. And with him went one of the most fascinating characters in our midst.

Oh, John was no saint. And if there were a move to canonize him, he'd be the first to go directly to the Vatican to file a complaint.

He was good at filing complaints. Once, he dyed his moustache and beard green and marched in the Minneapolis St. Patrick's Day parade. But only after filing a complaint that the parade sponsors didn't have a permit.

There was standing-room-only Monday at a memorial service for John in St. Peter's Catholic Church of Mendota, his boyhood town. Then there was a celebration at the nearby Mariner, complete with music by the Hall Brothers jazz band. A sad affair would have offended John.

"Laughter was what his world was all about," said his wife, Carol.

When John laughed, everybody laughed, but mostly John laughed at himself.

I first met John, of Hopkins, when he was running for a House seat in the Minnesota Legislature. He weighed 270 pounds, stood 6 feet 3, had a white mustache and beard, red sideburns and patches of brown in his long yellow hair.

He had proclaimed himself, at 53, "The World's Oldest Hippie," and wore psychedelic overalls, a turtleneck sweater and a huge peace necklace.

John's platform for running for the Legislature was simple: "If elected, I will do my best to abolish my legislative seat. There are too many guys over there doing nothing now." He actually got beyond the primary.

When asked why he initially decided to run for office, he said: "My relief lady says I should get a job."

To point out the flaws in the system, John went on welfare that year, despite the fact he owned his own photography business and a home with a swimming pool.

"I figured, 'If I can get on relief, anybody can,'" he said. It lasted three months.

Each morning he would go to the welfare office and his "relief lady" would give him two job opportunities. "I go to each one and they take one look at me and turn me down," John said. "Then the relief lady would give me food stamps."

He got caught when they checked his bank account. "But I learned something: When on relief you lose your privacy and your dignity. The only relief one gets from relief is when one gets off relief."

Earlier, John took a red-white-and-blue ax and went to a judiciary committee room at the Legislature. He offered to "break down the door." It was done in opposition to a "no-knock" clause in a bill to allow police more powers in entering houses unannounced.

He got into it one time with the medical world. He and Carol had a baby boy, whom they dearly loved. The boy developed a medical problem, not serious.

A doctor said it would cost $250 to cure the boy. John was outraged at what he considered a high price.

February 2, 1975

ROBERT T SMITH

"I told him the baby originally cost $225 to be born, so I would like to trade him in on a new one instead of getting the old one fixed. It would save twenty-five dollars.

John was against war (although he fought in Africa and Europe during World War II), racism, insurance companies, organized religion and the Federal Reserve System. And bugs. He hated them. Long before the Metrodome, John domed his swimming pool to keep out the bugs.

He always said he had read only three things in his life: the *Rubaiyat* of Omar Khayyam, George Orwell's *1984* and *TV Guide.*

And he had a thing about oatmeal: "If everybody would eat oatmeal, we would have a better world. There would be peace and happiness." He never really explained that.

During his political campaigns, he had a poster with his photo on it and the words beneath: "Don't Trust Anyone Under 30." He would greet crowds at his speeches with: "I'm glad to see it's such a small crowd. 'Cause I lose 80 percent of the people by my appearance alone."

John wasn't always so zany. He was pretty straight until about 1960 when "my kids taught me a new way of life." And, he said, a heart condition helped.

John had some brushes with the law. But he never spent a day in prison. He once was convicted of mail fraud, but the conviction was dismissed because of a faulty witness. He was charged with assault and battery involving a man in a downtown Minneapolis phone booth, but that, too, was dismissed. He got off on some traffic violations by claiming he didn't get out of his car when police stopped him because of "police brutality." He said he had read in the newspapers about it. Never mind it was in New York. He said he stayed in the car until more police arrived so there would be witnesses to any brutality. Judges seemed to believe John.

His latest caper last autumn involved a car insurance company. Because of a minor accident, the company canceled his insurance, his wife's and a son's. John complained to the state: "I see that I must divorce my wife, disown my son and change my name."

John had two open-heart surgeries, and that was too much for him.

I'm going to miss John. He fought the world with imagination and humor. Mostly, like Don Quixote, he lost. But the world needs men like John.

February 2, 1975

A bewildered boy gets help

A scene at a Minneapolis Red Owl supermarket . . .

A small slightly built boy of about 7 was doing the shopping for his mother and little sister. The Red Owl check-out clerk said the boy doesn't have a father and his mother works.

He had put several items in his cart, but he couldn't read part of the note his mother had given him. He got to the check-out counter and there was a long line behind him.

"Could you read this for me?" he asked the young girl clerk.

There were some grumbles from those waiting behind the boy. But the clerk studied the note a minute and said the only thing the boy didn't have were three small turkey pot pies.

The boy looked a little bewildered.

"C'mon," said the clerk and she took him to the aisle and found the pies.

The lineup became more disgruntled. Some left and got into other lines. Their places were taken by other shoppers.

"Well, for heaven's sakes," said one middle-aged woman.

"You'd think we had nothing to do but stand in lines all day," said an irritated man.

An elderly woman wearing a blue stocking cap waited patiently. She had what you often see in the carts of the elderly: a half pound of hamburger, not ground beef; a small loaf of day-old bread, a small can of applesauce and a bag of the kind of coffee you grind yourself.

There were bare leather streaks on the fur collar of her coat. There was a hole in the finger of one of her mittens.

ROBERT T SMITH

March 23, 1975

When the clerk and the auburn-haired boy returned, a thin, nervous woman in line said: "Maybe now we can get some service here." She pushed her cart up against the man in front of her.

The clerk totaled the boy's groceries and presented him with the bill. He reached into his jacket pocket and came up with nothing.

"What now?" asked a man.

The boy blushed and he searched other pockets. Others left the line. But with newcomers the line remained about the same.

From his right rear pants pocket the boy found the food stamps. He smiled and handed them to the clerk.

"I'm sorry," said the clerk, "but you're a dollar seventy-three cents short."

"This could go on forever," said the middle-aged woman. The boy blushed again and was frightened. He wouldn't look at anybody.

"That's all I've got," he said. "And my mother's not home yet from work."

A further exodus from the line. A man and woman tangled their carts as they moved to another check-out counter.

The elderly woman with the blue stocking cap left her cart and went forward to the young clerk and the boy.

"Give him his groceries and I'll take care of it," she said.

The boy smiled and in a few minutes was out the door. At 7, you don't always remember to say thank you. Especially when you want to hurry away from something.

When it was the elderly woman's turn to check out, she also paid the $1.73 for the boy. With her food stamps.

March 23, 1975

Without a book, she felt naked

For 80 years she lived in the worlds of Walt Whitman and Mark Twain and Shakespeare and Gertrude Stein. Now she is dead and, as one friend said, God better love books.

Vivien Barrett taught us kids in the neighborhood what a book was. We had all learned to read in school, beginning to pride ourselves because we had advanced beyond "Run, Skip, Run."

But climbing trees in a nearby "jungle" and mastering the little hills on short skis that we held to our feet by rubber bands cut from inner tubes were much more fascinating than sitting around with some old book.

Vivien lived across the street from where I grew up in southwest Minneapolis. She was the mother of a good friend, Tom Barrett. She always, in my eyes, resembled Katharine Hepburn—tall and sometimes stern and sometimes angry, but always spirited.

It seemed that every time I looked, she was sitting by the front window of her home with a book. Nobody in the block had any money and I know she cleaned and cooked like the rest of the mothers. But she lived in Paris and Moscow and Oz and Wonderland and 12th-century England and on the islands of Greece, even though she never left the United States.

"Come here, young man," she beckoned one day. "You must be 10 or 11 now. And it's time for you to learn to read."

"But I can read," I protested.

"You can run your eyes left to right on a page and maybe even comprehend a bit," she said. "But reading is a way of life. They don't teach it in the schools these days." Until she died recently, she maintained they don't teach reading in the schools.

She read me a little poem by G. K. Chesterton. It was about the donkey and how ugly and useless an animal he is. It ended by telling that there was, however, a day when for one donkey there were "shouts about his ears" and "palms before his feet."

"Marvelous, isn't it?" asked Vivien.

It left me cold. I didn't understand, and it apparently was obvious.

"But think, young man," said Vivien. "What happened on that day?"

I thought and then, not being too swift, I got it. Palm Sunday. Jesus rode into Jerusalem in triumph—on a donkey.

It doesn't sound like much, but it was the first time I had unraveled something that wasn't direct and obvious. I have never forgotten that initial flicker of translation of something other than Jack and Jill.

There followed many an afternoon or evening with Vivien, who read from her seemingly endless supply of good books. She began with stories she knew we would like the most—the tales of Robert Louis Stevenson. She never was too impatient to stop and explain if there was a passage we didn't understand.

"It is better to learn one thing new than to read 1,000 pages that you have no trouble with," she would say. We would sometimes spend an hour or more on one paragraph in *Ivanhoe*.

Vivien never flaunted her knowledge. She couldn't care less about impressing people with her intimate relationship with many of the world's great writers. And she never felt she herself could write.

"If I thought I had a talent for writing, I'd quit reading and get to it," she said.

To us kids, Vivien seemed different. She wasn't like the other mothers in the neighborhood. You figured she knew things that nobody in the whole world could guess. And she appeared to be constantly amused by some great secret joke.

Because of her, I traveled with Gulliver and the Jukes' family and fought with Robin Hood and Richard the Lionhearted and fell in love with Cathy of *Wuthering Heights* and Cyrano's Roxanne and Eliza Doolittle long before *My Fair Lady*.

We buried Vivien Barrett next to her husband in Fort Snelling National Cemetery. The priest talked about learning to live with sorrow and about life after death.

I didn't hear much of what he said. I was thinking of a tall, slender woman who felt naked without a book in her hand.

May 5, 1975

Danny Kaye: laughs for sick kids

There were five kids in the ward at L'Hopital de St. Pierre in Paris. They all were seriously ill.

It was the fall of 1967 and I was there to do a story on French hospitals for *Time* magazine. Part of it involved facilities for children.

The mood of the ward was about as cheery as death row. The five kids just rested on their beds—no noise, no complaining. Just nothing.

Four of them were French, and one was a slightly-built German boy. The ward had few windows, and the darkness fit the mood.

And then a lean, red-haired man swept into the room. He was wearing a beret four sizes too large. It flopped over his ears.

He carried a walking stick with one of those bulb-horns attached.

"Bonjour, mes amis," he said in a bass voice that suddenly rose to a falsetto. Then he squeezed the bulb and the horn sounded.

The five children laughed. The whole ward seemed to brighten.

It was the only time I saw Danny Kaye in person. He wasn't traveling with a full entourage. He was alone.

The Jewish boy from Brooklyn began to speak his kind of French. It was all fake, but done in a perfect accent. The kids howled.

Kaye discovered the German boy, so he did the same act in German. No one was to be left out.

One French girl held out her hand. Kaye bounced over to her bed, gently took her hand and kissed it—all the while jabbering in his phony French.

She got caught up in it, and promptly became a fine lady, mimicking a snooty grand dame.

Then the other four kids held out their hands. Kaye did a stint with each one.

"S'il vous plait, une chanson," begged one French boy.

Kaye knew that meant a song. He left the ward a moment and returned with a guitar. He sang "Yankee Doodle Dandy," accompanied by funny faces and pratfall dancing.

The kids now were going all out. The difference in mood was striking.

Kaye stayed about an hour. Then he said "Au revoir" and started to leave. The kids begged for one more song. They got it.

The entertainer had seen me earlier, but never broke stride. Now, we were walking out together. I introduced myself, and told him why I was there.

"Do me a big favor," he said. "Don't write about this. The kids will think I came just so I could get my name in *Time*."

I promised, and kept it. But, now that he's dead at 74, I figured it would be all right to tell the story.

As he left me that day in Paris, I asked him where he was going.

"There are two more Paris hospitals with kids in them," he said, and disappeared.

August 13, 1975

The buzzards at least are honest

You sit on the huge dark rocks of the North Shore of Lake Superior. It's the kind of vacation without stress and go-go, the kind where the cool air sweeps out your mind.

You're at Solbakken Resort, just north of Lutsen, Minn., a non-fancy, non-take-advantage-of-the-traveler place, with the healthy birch trees and the fir and pine and that rocky shore that prefaces a lake that has all the fascination of a sea.

You throw some broken bits of bread a few yards ahead of you, and you watch the human comedy of the sea gulls.

From a nearby rock jetty, seven mostly white sea gulls with gray wings set sail, slowly, carefully toward the prize. No guts, though. They seem to be willing to wait, perhaps until death, for a crumb of bread.

You think of all the people you know who are waiting. With no guts. Perhaps until death.

And then from the sun comes a lone, brave sea gull. No, not Jonathan. Just one who may be more desperate than the others.

The brave one swirls to a landing, snaps up a piece of bread and flys back into the sun. Four of the waiters take after, try to attack in mid-air, to steal from their own what they hadn't the nerve to acquire.

You think the buzzards at least are honest.

But the brave one has changed things. He or she, after all, did get a crumb without retaliation. So three of the waiters circle the remaining crumbs, slowly getting closer.

They land, and begin to profit. Then the rest come immediately. The Gold Rush. The Uranium Drive. A wildly, bullish stock market.

Ah, but along comes a grayish-brown sea gull. A loud squawk, a feinted beak attack. The waiters flee, mostly losers. The grayish-brown one, the stronger, smarter, johnny-come-lately takes over.

Grayish-brown finishes the crumbs. Nothing left. And then, in wisdom, leaves.

August 19, 1975 — ROBERT T SMITH

But the waiters are joined by eight more. There is nothing left, but they wait for nothing.

You think of the people you know. The brave ones who are unpopular. The ones with power, who take advantage of it. And are never satisfied. And, mostly, you think of the waiters.

It's dusk, and the rocks become a light maroon. The waiters still are waiting for nothing. And, you know, that after they've had enough of waiting for nothing, they will leave for the nearby rock jetty.

To do it again.

August 19, 1975

She wanted to die alone . . .

She was a woman of dignity. And when at age 72 her doctor told her she had a terminal illness, she decided to leave her family and friends and die alone.

The tall, erect Minneapolis woman wanted them to remember her as tall and erect and dignified. She had some money and decided to go to a small village in Brittany on the west coast of France.

There were some protests from friends and family, but the elderly woman remained firm. While in France, she wrote letters to the friends and family. They were warm, sometimes almost caustic, but in no way maudlin.

To a young grandson, she wrote: "You haven't the sense that God gave you—at least not yet. But you're a cheerful fellow and you've got spirit. The sense may come later . . ."

To a man who had been her friend for 40 years, she wrote: "You're next, you old goat. But don't fret about it. Once you know, it isn't bad at all. I guess that worrying that it may happen some day is worse than it happening. Remember to wear your muffler in the winter . . ."

The woman told about the sea and the flowers of Brittany and of some potato farmers she had befriended. "We have a spot of wine together occasionally at the local bistro," she wrote. "I've picked up a bit of street French, and I'm actually beginning to understand them."

At one point, she wrote a sort of general letter that she mailed to them all: "If you think I'm going to give you a lot of sage advice, you're wrong. I really don't have much. It's been my experience that people don't learn from anything but experience anyway."

A daughter in Minneapolis said her mother had always enjoyed little quips.

"She was really against being mushy or sentimental. But she cared," the daughter said.

Two weeks ago, the family and friends got word that the woman had died. As she wished: alone and with dignity.

September 15, 1975

A doctor for all reasons

While delivering the baby of an unwed mother, Dr. Henry Van Meier sings "Love, Love, O Careless Love." But chances are he sends no bill.

Henry sometimes wears a beanie with a propeller on it, and says of medicine: "God gets them well and I get paid for it."

The second son of a man who Henry knew well was born. Henry told the man this one was "on the house." When a fifth child was born, also a boy, the man yelled in jest down the hospital corridor: "You're fired, Henry, you promised a girl."

Henry yelled back: "Don't blame me, you sex maniac."

The delightful Dr. Van Meier is 74 and has been a family physician in Stillwater since 1928. He is an excellent doctor and a fine human being, but not the type to be promoted by the American Medical Association.

If he does not live up to the AMA image, no one in Stillwater seems to care. He still does a brisk business and is well respected, as well as loved.

One day he was in a Stillwater cafe run by Sam Crea, executive director of the Variety Club of the Northwest. It was the cafe's opening night. Henry had a cup of

ROBERT T SMITH   September 15, 1975

coffee and gave Sam a crumpled-up bill. A $500 bill. Sam tried to give it back, saying Henry had done it inadvertently.

"Ring it up and, dammit, when I want a cup of coffee, put it on my tab," said Henry. It was his way of helping the new cafe survive.

Born in Huron, S.D., Henry first thought he might become a preacher, as his father wished. But one day he was fishing for bullheads. Unknown at the time to Henry, his father was standing nearby. Henry's line became snarled and he let out some expressive language. Recalls Henry: "That night at supper my father said: 'Henry, I think you'd better become a doctor.'"

He graduated from the University of Minnesota medical school and, after a short stint at Glen Lake Sanitorium, settled in Stillwater. He now occupies a 19th-century building on Myrtle St.

The elderly physician still makes house calls day or night. One night a week ago, he was called at 11 p.m. He went out. He came back about 1 a.m. and got another call at 1:30 a.m. He went out again.

"I got to sleep about 3 a.m. and then had to get up at 6," he said. Why? "I never miss 'Sunrise Semester' on the television," he said.

There are a hundred stories of Henry not only working for nothing, but helping people in other ways. Henry will not talk about them. "We eat," is his comment on how much money he takes in.

Henry also is interested in the emotions as well as the body. "There is one key question to ask patients when they complain about feeling lousy," said Henry. The question: "Do you awake in the morning more tired than when you went to bed?" If yes, Henry starts in on the emotions.

He will chat kindly and friendly like if he feels that is needed. Or he can be tough. A man came in one morning, said he felt terrible and demanded that Henry do something. Said Henry:

"You cut out those (expletive deleted) cigarettes and take about 50 pounds off your big fat behind and then come and ask for help if you need it." The man did what he was told and is alive and well today.

There are three things Henry believes are necessary for a good life. One: "Keep your ass off your shoulders. You may not be that big. Know who you are, and stop playing roles."

Two: "There are two important three-word sentences. 'I love you. I don't know.'"

Three: "Don't hate anybody."

He has a mischievous spirit too. One time the Stillwater Lions Club was upset because the restaurant where they met served dull food. Henry created "Great Aunt Lucy Day" and told the restaurant manager she was a relative of the president of Lions Club International. The food was superb. After the dinner, Henry gave a 20-minute speech on the fictional Aunt Lucy.

Or the time Henry was in Sam's cafe. Sam, a good friend, was telling some strangers that Henry was weird and that he had been unfrocked as a doctor for unusual behavior. Henry in the meantime left the cafe.

People who overheard Sam's statements hurried to assure the strangers that Henry was a fine doctor and well-respected.

Henry entered the cafe wearing his beanie-with-propeller and carrying a plumber's bag and a large monkey wrench.

"Did somebody call about a sick rhinoceros?" asked Henry.

October 16, 1975 ROBERT T SMITH

Lilli Palmer, fragile, quiet and beautiful

A former wife of Rex Harrison was in town Monday. So was a close friend of the late Noel Coward and Laurence Olivier and Gary Cooper. So was a very fine actress and now an author. They all are Lilli Palmer.

At 61, she still has that European charm that made us fall in love with her in movies such as *Cloak and Dagger* and *Counterfeit Traitor.* And she still is a fragile, quiet and beautiful woman.

She is on a national tour promoting her book, *Change Lobsters—And Dance,* published by Macmillan. It is her autobiography from her childhood in Berlin, through her hectic 15-year marriage to Harrison and up to the serene present.

A Jew, Ms. Palmer fled Germany at the age of 18. "In a way, that was lucky," she said. "I found myself without a home, without a country and without a job. I had to start a new life, and it turned out to be a fascinating one."

The actress said she fell in love with Gary Cooper at the age of 11. "And when I came to Hollywood in 1945, he was my first American leading man," she said.

There are two kinds of actors, she said. "One is the superb, highly trained actor, such as Olivier, Tracy and Bogart. The other is the nonactor, the personality, such as Cary Grant or Clark Gable or Cooper." She quoted Cooper as saying: "Acting is a cinch. I just learn my lines and try not to bump into the furniture."

Ms. Palmer said that she had decided not to write much about "Henry Higgins" Harrison, but that he wrote about their marriage and "it was mostly a fantasy." She was his wife during his affairs with Carole Landis, who committed suicide, and Kay Kendall, who died of leukemia.

"Rex was a man who wanted his cake and eat it too," she said. "He admitted it. I just thought that period in his life would pass. But then Kay became ill and Rex felt he had to marry her."

Then, she said, he asked a strange favor. "He begged me to promise to re-marry him after Kay was dead," she said. "I told him that I had met a wonderful man (writer Carlos Thompson) and was going to marry him. Rex said that was OK, but I had to divorce Carlos and remarry him when the time came."

For three years Ms. Palmer played along, writing Harrison regularly. "Then Noel Coward got angry with me," she said. "'Who do you think you are, Florence Nightingale?' he said. I wrote Rex and told him 'no deal.'"

Ms. Palmer and husband Thompson now live in the Swiss mountains. She said she is still making films in Europe, has a television show in Switzerland and plans another book.

Perhaps the most poignant part of her book is an account of the death of Coward. About 200 people had come from throughout the world for a last party—including Olivier, David Niven, Lerner and Loewe, Burt Bacharach, Marlene Dietrich. That night Coward sat at the piano for the last time.

"For a while, he just stared at the keyboard. Then, hesitantly, he raised his frail hands and struck a few chords. In a high, almost inaudible voice, he began to sing.

"When he came to the words of that most famous 'The most I've had is just . . .,'

ROBERT T SMITH　　　　　　　　　　　　**January 10, 1976**

he paused for a moment looked slowly around the circle of people, smiled, and continued, 'a talent to amuse . . .'"

As she said, a most fascinating life.

January 10, 1976

He pleads guilty with pleasure

Not often does a man plead guilty in court . . .

Harry H. Peterson is a friend of mine. He's 93 now, and until his retirement had quite a career in the law.

He formerly was Minnesota's attorney general and, for some time, was a Minnesota supreme court justice. He unsuccessfully ran for governor of this state in 1950.

Recently, he told me about Clarence, a quiet, distinguished man who lived in Minneapolis. He was a widower of reasonable wealth and a man of great pride.

Harry knew the man and was surprised when Clarence was accused in a civil suit of being the father of the as yet unborn child of a 22-year-old woman.

"I referred him to a very good lawyer," said Harry. "The lawyer told Clarence it was a piece of cake, that the case would undoubtedly be thrown out of court."

The idea was that Clarence would take the stand and it would be his word against hers. "You have a good reputation and so with a standoff we should win it easily," said the lawyer.

Clarence was very quiet during all this talk.

"I noticed that he didn't seem to be worried," said Harry. "He was interested in all that was said, but he somehow was detached from it all."

Harry and Clarence met several times before the case got into court. They had lunch or just spent some time in Harry's club in St. Paul.

"We talked about everything, but when it came to the trial, Clarence would clam up," said Harry. "He just didn't seem to be interested. I thought he was terrified and just didn't want to discuss it."

The woman was investigated by the lawyers defending Clarence, and they established that she had no "visible means of support" and assured Clarence they would attack her in court and, most certainly, would discredit her.

Clarence listened to everything, and then would say nothing.

The day of the trial arrived. Harry asked Clarence if he wanted some company at the courthouse in Minneapolis.

"He allowed as how that might be nice," said Harry. "So, I went. Not as a lawyer, but just as a friend."

Clarence had been carefully coached by his attorney. He would deny everything and then let his reputation stand against what was left of hers after his attorney got through.

There were preliminaries and a lot of usual legal stuff and then the Hennepin County district court judge asked what plea Clarence would like to enter.

"Not guilty," said the attorney of Clarence.

"Guilty," said Clarence.

Those in the courtroom, including Harry, not a man without cynicism, were shocked.

The attorney for Clarence asked for a recess and got one. But Clarence wouldn't budge. He was guilty, he said, and he wanted the world to know it.

Reluctantly, the attorney led Clarence back into the courtroom.

"My client insists he's guilty," said the attorney.

The judge found Clarence guilty and ordered him to make financial arrangements for the 22-year-old woman and the impending offspring.

"This has been most unusual," was the judge's only comment.

Clarence had dozens of copies made of the court order finding him guilty of fathering the child of the young woman. He sent them to all his friends.

Three days later, he celebrated his 90th birthday.

February 2, 1976

ROBERT T SMITH

A hug for a different little girl

I settled into the city bus for a ride to downtown Minneapolis. I always have a book when riding the bus. But this time I didn't get to read.

At 46th and Lyndale, a little girl scrambled onto the bus. She wore a pink dress with a white bow at the waist. Her hair was the color of spun honey. She was happy.

A woman, apparently her mother, put some coins into the fare box and they took a seat near the front. But sitting wasn't for this little girl.

She wanted to explore, to be friendly.

Down the aisle she came, stopping first by a well-dressed man who looked like he might be a stock broker. The girl, thinly-built, smiled and touched the man on his shoulder.

The man visibly flinched, grabbed up his newspaper and used it to block out the little girl.

She gazed at the man for a moment, then decided to continue her journey down the aisle.

I watched the other people on the bus. They suddenly became busy. Some looked out a window. Some began talking to the person next to them.

It was apparent they wanted no part of the little girl.

The woman who got on the bus with the girl was watching her. But she made no attempt to retrieve her. Apparently, she had been through the scene many times.

The girl stopped by a middle-aged woman and touched her face. The woman winced and, although gently, brushed the girl's hand away.

We are so afraid of some things in this country.

The girl approached a young woman, maybe 25, and said: "Hi." This woman managed an embarrassed "Hello," and looked like she would rather have been walking alone on Hennepin Av. at night.

You could measure the tension in the bus. It was the tightness that stems from ignorance and fear and, perhaps, embarrassment for having both.

The girl spotted a handsome man wearing a trench coat, and a three-piece suit.

She tried to climb onto his lap. He stiff-armed her with both his arms.

"I love you," she said.

He reddened and recoiled from the girl. It was as if she had just announced that he was about to contract a deadly disease. The young man turned his face to the window.

The girl was undaunted. She still was smiling and she continued her trek.

I had seen the reaction to such a girl many times, mostly as a reporter. To be honest, I had at first felt the same way. It took some education and understanding to correct such feelings.

Finally, the girl in the pink dress saw a small boy sitting on a woman's lap. She made her way toward him.

The boy, about 4 maybe, was not afraid. He smiled at the girl and did not turn his head away.

The girl stood by the boy for a moment. She didn't say anything, and one wondered if getting snubbed after her "I love you" had perhaps restrained her. No, not possible.

With a slow movement, the girl reached out and hugged the little boy. It was an open, warm, uninhibited embrace.

The little boy hugged back—the little retarded girl.

April 12, 1976

Glen Olson: the impractical joker

A very strange thing happened on the way to this meeting today which at this point reminds me of a story. The disturbing point of all this is that, through this bitter lesson, we should know better. I need hardly remind this astute audience, without fear of successful contradiction, that we hand down to posterity a few choice words about your splendid hospitality....

Glen Olson

Glen Olson is vice president of a big bank. He's also an imp, a man whose sense of

ROBERT T SMITH   April 12, 1976

humor is as subtle as a stiletto; a creative, inventive, impractical joker.

The words at the beginning of this column are part of a speech that Olson gives deadpan to various groups. It makes no sense, but people come up to him afterward and compliment him on giving a "great talk."

It continues:

We may be surprised for, above and beyond the clouds, we see the sunshine through. . . . As you all know, we face business on a day-to-day basis. . . . Experience teaches us that the future lies ahead. . . .

I've heard serious talks worse than that.

Olson, 61, a vice president of American National Bank, St. Paul, has been playing tricks on people for decades. He loves it. And he goes to great lengths to do it. Example:

A friend he hadn't seen for 30 years called him and told him he was coming to Minneapolis. Olson already had something in mind. He told the friend he couldn't meet him at the airport, but would show up at the hotel.

Olson then asked the Radisson to lend him a bellhop's uniform for a while.

The friend arrived and went to his room. "He's a cheapskate and I knew he'd carry his own bags," said Olson.

Olson arrived shortly, in uniform, with a tray of glasses. The friend was on the phone reconfirming return airline reservations. He didn't recognize the bellhop, who suddenly attacked his suitcase.

He found a bottle of scotch and poured himself a drink as the friend, still on the phone, watched him. Then the bellhop grabbed a freshly-pressed suit from the luggage and jammed it into a dresser drawer.

The friend began to get upset as the shenanigans continued, and then he tumbled to what was going on.

Then there's the bit at the bar. Olson used to be a traveling salesman and he liked to meet people. He knew all the bartenders on his route.

One trick he used in the bars involved putting a string in the corner of his mouth, running the string over one ear and down to this shirt pocket. In the pocket was a penlight with a red bulb.

Then he'd sip his drink. Others at the bar would become curious and the bartender would say that Olson was testing the reaction of martinis on his lower abdominal tract. If there was trouble, the red light would go on.

When no one was looking, Olson would put on the light. Soon, everyone at the bar would get excited and try to help the poor man with the lower abdominal problem. And soon, Olson would have some new friends.

The banker created an "answer box," which is guaranteed to ensure harmony in any household. It is a "computerized" device that answers all questions with two answers: maybe or no.

"When you're watching the Vikings, and the wife comes in and asks you to take out the garbage, you refer her to the answer box," said Olson.

He was born in Chippewa Falls, Wis., grew up in South Bend, Ind., and was a navy pilot in World War II. A trick helped him become a pilot.

Olson is 5 feet 6, and the minimum height for a navy pilot is an inch taller.

Olson checked out the physical exam area and noticed that the candidates had to take off everything but their socks. He went to a nearby drug store, got a bunch of half dollars and stacked them in his socks. He miraculously grew an inch.

He flew twin-engine attack bombers in the South Pacific, sitting on two pillows.

After the war, he had a series of selling jobs before settling down in St. Paul and eventually getting into banking. He also married Mary Kay and they have seven children.

"My biggest joy is to create laughter and fun," said Olson. "I think it's very important for your health." Example:

Bill Farmer, St. Paul newspaperman and radio personality, had decided to quit his newspaper job (he later got it back). Olson, a friend, decided to give Farmer a "testimonial lunch with all his friends."

Olson hired the huge Prom Center. He brought Farmer to the lunch. On the marquee of the Prom: "Farewell Party for Bill Farmer." As they entered, there were two women at the ticket tables, one with a sign marked "A to M," the other "N to Z."

The dining room tables were all set, and there was a head table with name cards on it: "Gov. Wendell Anderson," etc. Olson and Farmer took their seats at the head table.

When Farmer looked about, he saw two people in the audience, both at the far end of the room. They began to applaud, slowly.

Farmer laughed for 10 minutes, and Olson then took him to the real lunch at a restaurant.

There's a serious side to Olson. He is very much a family man, and he doesn't want his antics to hurt anyone. He also wants to dispel the idea that bankers are not human, although he admits that not all bankers love his tricks.

There was the time he went to a meeting of the Building Owners & Managers Association of Minneapolis, and unknown to them, showed a model of the new prison at Stillwater. He told them it would make a great new national headquarters for them, that the exercise yard would be just fine for tennis courts.

In conclusion, more of his famous speech.

We should pause and reflect for a moment on those pioneers in this room whose very presence today testifies with heartfelt thanks and unyielding determination....

And, in conclusion, I'd like to reiterate on the five most important points I've covered here today. Thank you.

June 22, 1976

URIS—absurd actors on diabolical stage

When Leon Uris, known throughout the world for his novels, arrived in Ireland, he was asked the must question: "Are you Protestant or Catholic?"

"I'm a Jew," said Uris, author of *Exodus, Battle Cry, Topaz, The Angry Hills* and *QB VII.*

"Ah, yes," said the Irish questioner. "But are you a Protestant Jew or a Catholic Jew?"

Uris told the story in Minneapolis the other day as he talked about his latest work, *Trinity, A Novel of Ireland,* which is No. 1 on the nation's best-seller lists.

Why did a Jew decide to spend three years traveling more than 10,000 miles in Ireland to write about what has caused Irishmen to kill each other for so long? "I saw parallels between the Irish and the Jews," said Uris. "The rabbis and the old Celtic scholars. David and his harp and the

ROBERT T SMITH

July 2, 1976

Irish harpists. And both the Irish Catholics and the Jews are struggling still to seek justice."

There's no doubt which side Uris is on. The Catholics represent one side of Uris's *Trinity,* described as "people longing for their freedom." Then there are the British, "who ventured to Ireland to conquer, colonize and exploit." The third leg represents the Scottish Presbyterians, "who were planted in Ulster to secure the crown's interests."

Uris spent time, however, with all three sides. "We went along in Belfast under all conditions," he said. Dangerous? "We could have been picked off by snipers at any time. Or kidnapped or assassinated. We were lucky."

Uris was charmed by the Irish as individuals. "It's a most beautiful country filled with people of wit and integrity," he said. "You can't help but love them."

Why do so many Americans not seem to understand the fighting in Ireland? "And they don't take it very seriously," said Uris. "For one thing, I don't think the media have done a very good job. There's a lot of reliance on British Information Office handouts.

"The battle in Belfast poses no threat outside of Ireland. It's not a world power struggle. In the Middle East there are interests for both the United States and the Soviet Union. But Ireland's troubles remain within its borders."

How do the Irish feel about Americans? "Just as both sides consider God is with them, both sides feel that the Americans are their allies," said Uris. "It's curious. Both sides get money from Americans and both sides love us."

The new novel does not deal with today's Ireland. It begins with the potato famine of the 1840s and ends with the Easter Rising of 1916. It's hero is a Catholic hill farmer turned soldier who has a love affair with a Protestant woman.

It is streaked with Irish philosophy, a mixture of reality and dreams. At one point, after much bloodshed, the hero says: "That is the cruelest joke of all, allowing myself to believe for a single crazy moment there was a life before death . . .

We are all absurd actors on the stage of the diabolical."

And why did Uris resort to the past to try to explain what is happening now in Ireland? Because, he said, he agrees with Eugene O'Neill who, in *A Moon for the Misbegotten*, wrote:

"There is no present or future—only the past, happening over and over again—now."

July 2, 1976

Poetic Bus Driver: "Don't fall on the mall"

Strut, man, strut,
as fierce as you please.
The nature of things
is to bring little kings
to their knees.   **Ben Shank**

As he wheels his bus along Minneapolis streets, Ben Shank is filled with thoughts of nature and love and irony and humor. Shank, 27, is a poet.

He has his light side, and enjoys creating little lines for his passengers on the No. 17 and No. 6 buses he drives for the Metropolitan Transit Commission.

In Downtown Minneapolis, it's not "Watch your step, please." It's: "Don't fall on the Mall."

And when a passenger wants to know what No. 6 buses go to Southdale, Shank will tell them D EJ and K will get them there. "Just remember," he says, "Donkey Eats a Jolly Kangaroo."

His sense of humor has produced little poems of imagination, such as his "Wild in the Bedrooms":

A zebra has fallen in love with my
*   Venetian blind*
soon enough he'll discover she's not
*   his kind . . .*

But Shank, 1805 W. Lake St., is mainly a serious poet. He graduated from the Raymond Experimental College at the University of the Pacific, Stockton, Calif. He

August 17, 1976

spent his junior year in Spain at the University of Madrid, during which he wrote a full-length play, *Dreams of Calgary*, in Spanish.

The native of Bronxville, N.Y., came to Minneapolis in 1971 to get a master's degree in industrial relations at the University of Minnesota. He has completed his work except for writing his thesis. It's difficult these days to make a living just on poetry, he says.

For three years he has been driving buses. "It was the last thing I thought I would do," he said, "but it's been great. I've met a lot of people, some of whom have been my best friends."

In one poem, he deals with the difference between his occupations. Part of it:

Simply because I'm on this fence
defending my right to straddle
between Art and Industry.

He pawns off on me
a certificate of saddle
from a distant university . . .

Shank has time for people, often people whom very few have time for. He tells about a bum who got on his bus on a Saturday morning a month ago:

"He had on army pants and a tuxedo top, with a ruffled shirt, and aviation glasses and a construction worker's hard hat. Everything was dirty. Kind of whacko." The derelict rode from downtown Minneapolis to Southdale. Ben took him into the shopping center for some orange juice.

"He wasn't exactly your ordinary Southdale shopper. A guard came by and my friend looked at him and said: 'Mornin', sheriff.' But they saw my uniform and apparently decided to leave him be."

And what is the bus-driving poet's main theme in his writing? "That love is the answer. People are muddling through a whole bunch of problems. The trick is to conjole them into a more loving frame of mind."

With, perhaps, "Tyranny of the Snapshot:"

The hungry camera is here somewhere
snapping at the holy and the hick . . .

But if you drive against the arrows, chums,
circle against the square,
When they open their albums,
you will not be there.

August 17, 1976

He laughed and smiled a lot—and yet . . .

We sat around the Bloomington home of a couple I know. Besides me, they had invited some teenagers from Randy's school and from the neighborhood.

The idea was to try to understand why he did it . . .

Randy, 16, was a sophomore at a private school. He laughed and smiled a lot, at least until recent months.

"You think you know your own kids," said Randy's father, Jeff. He didn't finish his thought.

I didn't know Randy well. But I learned some things about him in that Bloomington home. It only made it more of a mystery.

Randy did well in school, the worst mark he ever got was a B minus. He was a teacher's delight because, when a discussion would lag in the classroom, Randy would generate something again.

In a real way, he was into perpetual involvement. He made the freshman soccer team at school, and was student manager for the basketball team.

As a sophomore, however, he didn't go out for any sport.

An outgoing sort, at least on the surface, Randy liked to kid around, tell jokes and make people laugh. He seemed very friendly.

But one girl at the meeting said that Randy didn't have a close friend.

"He didn't have anybody he could really come across to," said the girl. "For one thing, I know he didn't have a girlfriend. Not a steady one, anyway."

Randy was not a discipline problem at school or at home. He was not into booze or drugs.

"We had our minor disagreements, but never anything serious," said his mother. "He was a reasonable boy . . ."

Randy, a medium tall lad with a stocky build, had times when he wanted to be alone. He liked to take long walks by himself. But nobody thought much of that.

"You know, I never saw Randy angry or upset," said a neighborhood teenager. "And he could always jolly you out of your snit or depression."

About a month ago, Randy was in shop class at school. He heated a tool until the tip was red. Then he burned "Goodbye" on a chunk of wood.

No one thought about that much. No one seemed to notice it.

Two weeks ago, Randy went to an afternoon movie with a teenage friend. They were walking home.

"You want to do something tonight?" asked the boy.

"Nah," said Randy, "I've got some things to do at home."

That night, Randy ate his dinner with the family. He was quiet for him. But no one thought about that much.

He excused himself and went to his room. He wrote four notes: one to his parents, and one each to his two sisters and brother.

There were no accusations in the notes. Nor bitterness. He mainly wrote about experiences they had shared, and told them how he felt about them.

And then he apologized. In the notes, he did not make clear why or for what he was apologizing.

"That sounds like Randy," said a girl at the meeting.

"He could be a bit mysterious at times," said a boy.

After writing the notes, Randy came downstairs and looked at his parents and sisters and brother. It wasn't a long look, and he said nothing.

Then he went back to his room, took his father's service revolver and put a bullet in his head.

He was dead before the family could get to him.

January 3, 1977

A wino with a heart

I have a friend who's tired of being tapped by winos for drink money. He's heard every line from "I need a bowl of soup" to "my children are dying of rickets." But the other day . . .

My friend, who wishes to be anonymous, is a well-to-do Minneapolis businessman. He's done some drinking himself, a source of irritation to his wife.

Not long ago, my friend and his wife were watching television. A public service commercial appeared with a man saying: "There are two alcoholics in every square block in the Twin Cities."

"Who's the other one?" asked my friend's wife.

That, of course, is a gross exaggeration, but it explains why he wants to be anonymous in this story.

My friend was walking down 4th St. toward Hennepin Av. the other day.

A wino approached him near the city hall. He asked for a half dollar.

"Is it soup for your dying kids?" asked my friend.

"It's neither," said the wino. "It's wine."

My friend was touched by such honesty, but he didn't feel he wanted to be touched for money.

Then my friend got an idea. He lied to the wino: "I don't have any money. My wife won't let me have any because she's afraid I'll buy booze with it."

The wino looked at my friend. "You mean, you ain't got nothing?" he said. "Your old lady won't give you even a quarter for a beer. That's heavy, man."

"But that's right," said my friend. "She says old John Barleycorn is my enemy."

"You wait right here," said the wino, who then went into a nearby liquor store. He came out with two bottles of wine and gave my friend one of them.

"Have a ball, pop," the wino said. Then he pulled out a wad of bills and gave my friend $5 for the future.

May 29, 1977   ROBERT T SMITH

For 21 years, a secret admirer

If all goes as usual, someone very early Monday morning will go to St. John's Cemetery at Jordan, Minn. When no one is around, that someone will place a bouquet of red carnations on the grave of a girl who died at 17.

If all goes as usual, it will be the 21st year that it's happened . . .

Judy Golda was a lively, involved girl. She was active in 4-H, and was president of the Jordan High School Junior class. She was a leader, but not a pushy, dominant person.

Judy cared about the students who were not leaders, those who had trouble with their studies and with their personal lives.

During her three years of high school, Judy played drums in the band. An art lover, she designed the murals for the 1955 high school prom. She won 4-H awards for cooking and baking.

On the night of April 18, 1956, Judy went to St. John's Catholic Church in Jordan—her church—for dress rehearsal of a play she was in.

After the rehearsal, about 11 p.m., she was in a car with other teenagers. They were traveling on Highway 169, about five miles southwest of Jordan, when they were rear-ended by a semi-trailer U.S. mail truck.

Judy and Joseph Woerdehoff Jr., 17, were killed. Three others in the car were critically injured. The Jordan Independent called it "one of the most tragic of human events in the annals of Jordan . . ."

There was a double funeral for Judy and Joseph the following Monday in St. John's church. They were buried in the church cemetery on a hill.

And every Memorial day since, there have been the red carnations.

"We have asked all our friends and relatives, but we've never been able to discover who the red carnation person is," said Judy's mother, Mrs. Marie Golda.

Judy's death was particularly painful to Marie and her husband, Lloyd, because, at the time, their son, Michael, was ill with kidney disease. They had been told that he would die, and three years later he did, at age 15.

Judy had a steady boyfriend at the time of the crash, but Mrs. Golda is convinced he is not the flower person. "We investigated that and there's no doubt that it is someone else."

At first, the Goldas were embarrassed by it. "I felt that I should know who the person is," said Mrs. Golda. "I couldn't understand why the secrecy."

For the Goldas and others in Jordan, it was reminiscent of the famed "lady in black" who, on each anniversary of the death of actor Rudolph Valentino, put flowers on his grave. Some feel that was some publicity stunt.

But Judy wasn't famous . . .

49

The Goldas always spent part of Memorial Day at Judy's grave, but never got a glimpse of the flower person. Always, the carnations were there before they arrived.

For a while, the Goldas were tempted to make a big effort to find the person, to maybe stay by the grave for the whole day.

But they had second thoughts. "If that's the way the person wants it, private and alone, then I feel that's the way it should be. We'll just stay curious."

And then she said: "It has been a great comfort to us to know someone else shares our loss and memories."

There is no chance the Goldas will meet the flower giver this Monday. They visited Judy's grave Friday, and left town.

September 11, 1977

He can't forgive . . . yet

About 2 a.m. Jan. 29, Shirley Snabb, 41, was shot in the back at close range with a 16-gauge shotgun. She died instantly.

The shooting occurred during an argument between Mrs. Snabb and Ralph C. Schluter in Schluter's home.

On Aug. 18, Schluter was found guilty of first-degree manslaughter by a Hennepin County District Court jury. He was sentenced up to 10 years in prison. There is an appeal.

Avron Snabb is a sensitive, thoughtful man, given to writing poetry. He would like to tell what it's like to suddenly lose a wife in a tragedy.

"I'd like the world to know we miss that woman," said Snabb, 43, who was there when the shooting occurred. "She had concern and love for her children and me."

Avron and Shirley met at Harrison Elementary School when he was 13 and she was 11. He had come from his family's farm at New York Mills, Minn., and she was a city girl.

They went to different high schools, but kept in touch. In all, they were married 22 years.

"After the shooting, there are the days of shock," said Snabb. "You don't do much

of anything. You kind of feel like giving up."

It was a week before he could enter their bedroom. "I slept on a couch." He left the disposition of her clothes to others. "There are so many little things that remind you. A pencil she used . . ."

The Snabbs had three children, two girls, now 18 and 21, and a boy, 14. "Shirley was a strict mother, but kind and loving," said Snabb. "She didn't cut off her love or concern for the children when they became adults at 18."

It was concern for her daughter that led to Mrs. Snabb's death. She, her husband and another man went to Schluter's home to take the daughter and another woman home. That's when the argument started and Mrs. Snabb was shot. She was a member of Abiding Savior Lutheran Church and went to Bible study sessions often. She was the family budget watcher and bookkeeper. "I haven't written a check in years," said Snabb.

After the initial shock, you pick up the pieces. "I realized that I was now both a father and a mother," said Snabb, whose three children still live at home. "There was so much loss and confusion. We had to reorganize."

Snabb, 2564 Sherwood Rd. NE., Mounds View, had long talks with the children. "I told them that they would have to help, to do the things that their mother had done," he said. "And they were great. It was as if they knew how much I needed their help."

There were immediate things to be done. Cancel their long-planned vacation trip to Florida. Get involved with the money, and writing checks again. Checking into Social Security death benefits. "Those are aimed toward the man dying first," said Snabb. "When it's the woman, there is a lot of paperwork and less money."

Mrs. Snabb had been working when she could at a fast-food restaurant. "She wanted to build a college fund for the kids," said Snabb, a design engineer for Bemis Co., Inc. Now there will have to be another way for college.

Snabb wanted to keep his young son busy. "I figured if he was active it would be easier." The father got the boy doing projects around the house. He encouraged him to deliver newspapers.

"Until it happens, you don't realize how much you lean on a spouse," said Snabb. "You just take it for granted."

There were bad times, like Mother's Day. They went to their church. Snabb had written a poem about his wife. The minister read it.

There was July 9, their wedding anniversary. "I sent the kids away for that day," said Snabb. "I spent the time alone."

Many people offered Snabb condolences. He appreciated that. But it was a former employer who maybe helped the most. He sent a short note, saying: "Hang in there, Av." That meant a lot to Snabb.

Mrs. Snabb loved camping and especially fishing. They had a lake cabin. "I sold the pontoon boat and didn't renew my fishing license," said Snabb. "It took a lot for me just to go to the cabin." And then, ironically, it had been broken into and things were stolen—including all the fishing equipment.

Then came the trial. "That opened it all up again," said Snabb.

There lingers the problem of bitterness. "Yes, I'm still bitter," said Snabb. "I have talked to my minister and a parish worker and they tell me I must forgive. But I can't yet . . ."

September 14, 1977

And now, a rock and a cloud to go

Can a little boy, not yet 2, love a tree? I don't know for sure, but I believe Bryan did . . .

Bryan, our son, plays a lot on the open front porch. Right next to it was a huge elm. It was maybe 45 years old, and actually was three trees that got together with a common lower trunk.

The boy saw his first bird in that old tree. He also was fascinated by the squirrels that took sanctuary there when they were somehow threatened. And he would trace the sun patterns on the porch floor— patterns made as the light passed through the leaves and branches.

Bryan would go up to the tree and pat it on the back, like a father giving approval to a child. He couldn't even say the word "tree." He still can't. But he knew the word, and would point at the old elm if you said it.

We got the notice not long ago. Our elm was a suspect for Dutch elm disease. I had read about the disease, but I figured that

was someone else's problem. Sort of like the cliché of sudden death: you figure it will never happen to you.

Even after the notice, we decided that they had made a mistake. The tree didn't look sick. There were a few scraggly branches, but there always had been. We, however, were about as realistic as Bambi. The tree was condemned.

It's only one of about 28,000 elm trees that will be destroyed by the end of this year. But this one was Bryan's.

The young men came with their truck and their tractor and their whining saws.

ROBERT T SMITH

December 4, 1977

Bryan was, at first, delighted with all the action. And then his mood changed. He would watch the men destroying his tree for a little while, then he would run away.

A bit later he would come back . . .

It reminded me of a short story I once read and loved. It was by Carson McCullers and involved a small boy and a wandering vagabond who liked his beer. I'll have Bryan read it one day.

The boy, delivering newspapers one cold morning, goes into a bar. The vagabond, who just arrived in town, calls the boy over and says: "I love you." The boy is frightened.

Then the tramp tells the boy about his life, and how he lost his wife because he didn't know how to love. He allowed as how love is a progressive thing, that you can't love a human being without the earlier experiences.

The tramp looks at the boy, then says: "First, you must learn to love a tree, a rock, a cloud . . ."

Bryan is not a moody boy. He's a funlover, and flows with curiosity about every new thing in life. He's the kind of kid who runs toward you with his arms up and open. He loves books, and brings them regularly to his mother, Janet, and me. He doesn't mind that we have read him the same books a dozen times.

With his good friend, Majel White, our neighbor who spends a lot of time with him, he goes to Lake Calhoun to feed the ducks and run barefoot in the water and laugh a lot.

After the elm was cut down, Bryan went over to the stump and patted it. He didn't cry. When you're not yet 2, maybe you figure the tree is not gone forever, that it will get well and come back.

But Bryan was quiet. The love of fun had left for a while. He missed his tree.

Majel gave us an idea: why not plant a new little tree in place of the elm, and let it grow up with Bryan?

That we're going to do, with Bryan present at the planting. He loved his old tree. Now he's only got a rock and a cloud to go.

December 4, 1977

The definition of a reporter

I walked into the huge, baronial mansion on St. Paul's Summit Av. a few nights ago. I could hear people inside talking and laughing. It was Paul Presbrey's funeral. And it was fun.

I had decided not to write about my old colleague, Paul, the consummate newsman who died recently. Perhaps I felt I knew too much about him. Or not enough. But what are you going to do when you have fun at a funeral?

The party was Paul's idea. He hated proper funerals, and would not even allow a memorial-service. I guess he had seen too many people die too violently. He donated his body to the University of Minnesota and everybody thought that was it.

But then the word came. Paul had decreed that there be a festive bash to consecrate his memory, with piles of food and enough booze to bring a rhinoceros to his knees. "I want to leave them laughing, or at least wondering," Paul told a friend.

The mansion was jammed with people.

November 22, 1978 **ROBERT T SMITH**

There were bankers and politicians and cops and lawyers and judges and media types and obscure, Damon Runyon-like characters that no one seemed to know. Except Paul.

Everyone seemed to be having a good time. They were telling Presbrey stories, some true, some myths and all of which I had heard before. "Did you hear the one about when Presbrey took a picture of a woman under a pile of bricks and then ran away without helping her . . ." Partly true. "What about the time he turned in a relative for murder . . ." True. "I heard that Paul once dressed up as a woman and got a scandal story involving an all-girl school . . ." False. But if he had needed to, he would have.

Paul Presbrey was a supremely skillful information gatherer who had a compulsion to get it to the public. The sleepless wonder exercised little discrimination in getting information. He just got it all.

If an editor turned a story down, Paul wouldn't give up. He'd try another editor and another. And, if all else failed, he would buttonhole people, as many as he could, and tell them the story personally. It was as if the information would burn his insides if he couldn't get it out.

I was city editor of the *Minneapolis Tribune* for about five years, and thus was Paul's boss. That's like being in control of one of those trick candles you blow out and within seconds it lights up again. You could never blow Paul out.

He never forgave me for not printing a story he titled, "The Second Virgin Birth." It was a true story, although not miraculous, and I judged it unfit for a family newspaper. I might as well have approved it, though, for Paul told it to everybody he met for the next 20 years. Two weeks before he died he introduced me to some of his cronies as "the man who turned down the second virgin birth." I also turned down "The Second Coming of Christ," another of Paul's enterprises.

Paul did not understand the word "no" when it came to getting a story. If a source denied him information, Paul would go around his end and get it somewhere else. He had, for instance, a ventilator shaft near a courtroom where he would go if it was decided to close the courtroom. That was years ago, of course. The shaft was big enough for two, and I went along once. You could hear just fine.

Paul was accused of being hardbitten and cynical. How ridiculous. At 67, he died naive. He was the town crier who never lost his enthusiasm for news. It's true he didn't get emotional about people and their problems. But it wasn't cynicism. It was just a part of him that was missing, even when he was very young, like being born with only one arm.

Whenever I think of Paul, I remember one night years ago when I was a young reporter. A big story broke in St. Paul, a multiple murder. The police radios were chattering about it.

I went to the night assistant city editor, Rolf Felstad, and said: "I guess I'd better get over there."

"No," said Rolf. "Presbrey's on it."

"But," I said, "it's late and near deadline and he could use help."

"No," said Rolf.

"But why?" I whined.

"I don't want you to get in Presbrey's way," said Rolf.

Later I realized the total confidence Rolf had in Paul. Rolf knew what I didn't then: that Paul was the definition of a reporter.

As I was about to leave the mansion, I overheard a veteran newsman say in regard to Paul: "You know, if there's life after death, we'll know soon." Yeah.

November 22, 1978

Place an anise bag around your neck

I first met Janet Flanner on a dreary spring day in 1964 in Paris. I was assigned to do a profile of the woman who for decades had written about Paris for *The New Yorker*.

She lived in a loft, formerly a maid's quarters, atop the Hotel Continental, near the Tuileries and the Palace de la Concorde.

When I arrived at the hotel, I asked for her at the registration desk. The clerk tele-

ROBERT T SMITH   November 22, 1978

phoned and she said she would come down. We were to have lunch.

Then I strolled in the center courtyard of the ancient hotel to look at the fountains and flowers.

Presently, a bellman came toward me, followed by a small woman. The bellman pointed me out to her and she approached and proclaimed:

"The next time you call on a lady, young man, either stay put or place an anise bag around your neck so I can follow the scent."

That did it. I was hers from then on.

Janet, who was 86 when she died recently in New York, loved to tell stories. And most of them were true.

She had come to Paris in 1925 from her straight-laced home in Indianapolis. Even as a young woman, she was a maverick, a person who honored puritanism, a person who didn't fit at all in Indianapolis.

So it was off to Paris where she soon fell in with others who could not cope with life in the United States: F. Scott Fitzgerald, Ernest Hemingway and Gertrude Stein, to name a few.

For hours, she would tell stories of such literary greats. Most of the tales were about personal experiences with them. There was the time she returned to her Paris apartment to find Hemingway in her bathtub, asleep with a rose in his navel.

There was the time Fitzgerald and Hemingway, with Janet present, argued over who was the best writer. There had been some drinking going on in that Paris cafe and the two began to shout at each other.

"I am," said Janet.

Both men laughed and the argument ended.

For 50 years she lived and wrote in Paris. She knew many of the famous in France: Albert Camus, Edith Piaf, Andre Gide, Colette, Jean Paul Sartre, Utrillo, Matisse, Picasso and others.

But, most of all, Janet knew Paris better than probably any other American. She took me to restaurants and bistros with marvelous food and entertainment. They were not listed in any tourist guides.

Her delight was to have a group of people for whom she performed. It wasn't that she demanded to be the center of attention, with her wit and storytelling. It just happened naturally.

I remember one night in a Paris cafe when she said she would tell us "the secret of life." We expected some profound statement revealing what mankind has sought since creation.

When she had our attention, Janet said:

"The secret of life, my friends, is to get out of Indianapolis." Then she laughed, her husky, throaty voice filling the room.

With style, humor and clarity, Janet chronicled Paris through a fascinating part of its history. She wrote a "Letter from Paris" under the pseudonym Genet. She would be sitting in the Opera one night to write about the debut of a new production. The next day, she would be in the Elysees Palace for tea with Charles de Gaulle.

And then, you would see the slight figure in Place Pagalle covering a particularly intriguing murder.

She told the Western world about Hitler long before most American journalists. She very early predicted his armies would one day conquer Paris.

"The French are in no way cowards,"

December 20, 1978   ROBERT T SMITH

she once told me. "But they are so interested in romance and beauty they have no time for war."

When it became apparent that her prediction was about to happen, Janet decided she would stay in Paris. "After all," she said, "I am really more French than most of the French."

Her editors and American government officials, however, thought it much too dangerous for the small lady to remain during the German occupation. With gentle force, they put her on a United States military plane.

As soon as the war ended, Janet was back on the Champs Elysees.

A story noting her death in the current *New Yorker* includes the following:

"Janet Flanner listened, hearing vibrations too delicate for the ordinary ear, and recording them for the rest of us. Her estimates of people and events, her perceptions and illuminations, were rarely embarrassed by time . . . Her domain was spacious, and anyone lucky enough to come her way—friend, acquaintance, passerby—was warmly invited to share it."

In the last two decades, one by one, Janet's friends died. Each death was more difficult for her than the one previous. Often, she would talk of her loneliness in that little loft, and finally, in 1975, after a half century in the city she loved, Janet returned to the United States.

She deplored the changes in Paris, the modernizations, the new, sleek, tall buildings, the influx of often-insensitive tourists.

"It's getting to be more like Indianapolis every day," she said.

December 20, 1978

Pete: Master of the pun

Pete the Printer, one of the 4th St. characters, is really frustrated these days. He is our local master of the pun and, a while back, his public outlet was terminated.

Pete, hardly at all known by his correct name, Edward D. Sjogren, was a frequent contributor to the *Minneapolis Tribune* when things such as puns were included in the Almanac.

That part of the feature was eliminated, but Pete has kept creating his puns. He's a friend, and as a Christmas present, I thought I might help out a bit.

It is said that punsters march to a different drummer, that they have a strange turn of mind that "sees" almost everything as a possible pun. Pete, owner of The Printers on 4th St., fits that perfectly.

Here are some of his latest creations:

This bar is called 'The Arthritis,' because it's such a painful joint.

Some people have a fetish for numbers. Seven is lucky, 13 is unlucky. Not me, I don't believe in it. I'm an eightheist.

Some of my stuff is freedumb of thought.

I always thought clone was something you sprinkled on yourself to smell good.

Pete, who reads Balzac and paints in oil, hates sports. He says: "The best thing about baseball is that it's not played in the snow." And to him Foreman is the boss of a printing shop. Ah, but some more of his puns, judged of course by how violently you whince:

There's gonna be a bullfight on television. It will be shown on "The Wide World of Snorts."

Some lawyers are known to be turn quotes.

John Smith asked a friend if Doubleday invented basketball. Said the friend: "Nay, Smith, that was baseball."

About our recent election: "'Tis said some voters were in Short supply."

"It's a disease," said Pete, referring to his addiction to puns. "Some folks look at the world through rose-colored glasses. I look at it through words. Ridiculous."

If it is a disease, in Pete's case it's incurable. And a punster without an outlet is like a stopped-up tea kettle.

"I used to watch people when they read my puns in the Tribune," said Pete. "The sight of their agony was a delight."

Some more agony:

Musicians who have beri-beri hope for jam session.

A friend was telling of his son who worked in a cemetery as a crew member, and was looking for a better position. He was told there would be an opening soon. "The sooner the better," he said, "as I am going in the hole."

And a final one he obviously wrote about himself:

North of here there's a group of word players. They call themselves "The Canadian Pun Set."

Merry Christmas, Pete.

December 24, 1978

John Gutowski— Mr. Auditorium

When Frank Sinatra arrived at the Minneapolis Auditorium some years ago, he was greeted by John Gutowski.

"Hiya, Mr. Sinister," said John. Sinatra loved it.

Last year Leonard Slatkin, artistic director of the Minnesota Orchestra's Viennese Sommerfest, conducted the orchestra's annual Guarantors Concert for 20,000 people in the Minneapolis Auditorium. It was a great success and as Slatkin stepped offstage to head for his dressing room, John Gutowski patted him on the back, and said: "Nice going, Slats."

Bewildered but pleased, Slatkin told some friends later: "Slats—that man called me Slats. He called me Slats!"

When Jimmy Carter was president and visited the auditorium, he was surrounded by Secret Service men who elbowed everyone out of the way—as usual.

Carter spotted Gutowski standing by a wall, with his arms held out. The president headed for John and they had a big bear hug.

A similar thing happened when Richard Nixon, then president, arrived at the auditorium. And when Lyndon Johnson did, and when John F. Kennedy did.

Who is John Gutowski? He's Mr. Auditorium, known by thousands of people who have attended events ranging from the old Minneapolis Lakers to ballets to circuses to conventions.

For 33 years, he has been part of the auditorium—an usher, a ticket-taker, a janitor. Now, he's called a floorman, which means he does whatever is necessary. But mostly, he says, he's been a people man.

"I enjoy people," he says. "I love them. It's a lot of fun dealing with 'em. Everybody's different."

John certainly is different.

He was born in north Minneapolis and went to De La Salle High School, but had to leave to help the family financially.

He and Mary have been married 48 years. They have three daughters and a son. In 1950, John was working at a furrier's and decided to take a second job, part-time at the auditorium. He's been there since.

There were times when he would not get home from the auditorium until 4 in the morning, and then had to show up at the furrier's at 8. He always made it. In his 33 years at the auditorium, he has missed only 10 working days.

On Oct. 7, John will become 70. He can't work for the auditorium after that.

Mandatory retirement. It means a big part of his life will be gone.

He can work for outfits that book events in the auditorium, and some of them already have contacted John. They don't want their customers to miss Mr. Auditorium.

Gary Dorrian may miss John the most. He's manager of the auditorium and knows the multiple value of a man like John.

There was the time the Russian ice

December 25, 1978

ROBERT T SMITH

show was at the auditorium and the technicians who came along spoke nothing but Russian.

"John spoke Polish, which is not too far away, and he served as our interpreter."

The same thing happened with a Polish dance group that wanted something special to eat. No one knew what they were saying except John.

"They want hot dogs," he said.

Dorrian particularly remembers a time when a motorcycle gang decided not to leave the auditorium at closing time. They were mean and had been drinking a lot of beer.

Along came John, and in a few minutes, the gang got up laughing and smiling and left without a problem.

"I'm not afraid of anybody," says John, who is most of 5 feet 7. "But if people act funny, I act funny with them. I like to get a step ahead of them, too."

He has dealt with teachers and doctors and lawyers and clowns and he treats them all alike. They seem to love it. People who come to the auditorium after an absence of five or 10 years ask for Little Johnnie. They remember.

Dorrian said: "He's the best thing we've ever had here. Genuine. Humorous. Concerned."

December 25, 1978

They really want Christmas to end

To those who will spend today within a loving family, this column is not dedicated. It's for those who are anxiously waiting for Christmas to end.

It is dedicated to the senior citizens who have no family and who will spend today much more aware of their loneliness.

It is dedicated to the poor who, contrary to the belief of some, do not experience miracles this time of year but who are much more aware of their poverty.

It is dedicated to the young who are having problems with their parents. Some are in foster homes, some in runaway homes, some in correctional institutions, some still at home. For them, this is not the season to be jolly.

It is dedicated to their parents, many of whom will spend today wondering where their children are. Or not caring where they are.

It is dedicated to the men and women in our prisons who will be locked up most of the day because the prison staff members will be home and thus security will be at a minimum. And especially to those inmates who haven't had a visitor since they entered the prison and who keep telling themselves they don't care.

It is dedicated to the families who will get together and go through the motions of a merry Christmas, but who will feel hypocritical about it—or should.

It is dedicated to all the alcoholics and other drug-dependent people who are piling it on especially heavily so that they will somehow survive until Wednesday. Or so that they may not survive.

It is dedicated to all the mentally and emotionally disturbed people who have been abandoned by everybody because it is difficult to be around them—particularly at this time of year.

It is dedicated to those who get depressed and belligerent this time of year and account for the fact that, between Dec. 4 and Dec. 26, there are more broken jaws than at any other time of the year. So reports the various orthodontists' associations.

It is dedicated to all the lonely who live in hotels and rooming houses and apartments—and the lonely who live within a family. What must they think of the television commercials showing actors playing members of happy families opening their after-shave lotion or perfume?

And, finally, it is dedicated to a man born 2,000 years ago who felt for all these people.

ROBERT T SMITH January 17, 1979

Smiths: Never a president

There are 2,180,960 of us in this country. We could replace the total populations of Minneapolis and St. Paul twice and have a lot left over. There are enough of us to more than populate any one of 18 states.

We are Smiths.

Anyone without the name Smith, the most common in the United States, has no idea what a burden it is.

When I was in the fourth grade at Riley School there were six Smiths in my class—three of them were named Robert, like me. The teacher ended up calling us by numbers, No. 1, No. 2, No. 3. I was 3.

I once portrayed a pink daisy in a school play. It was my big chance for some recognition, but Smith No. 2 got all the credit. He wasn't even in the play.

I have never quite forgiven my father for naming me Robert. At the time of my birth, Robert was even more common than it is now—if that's possible. My mother wanted my first name to be Tighe, her maiden name.

Father said the kids might tease me with such a name. So he gave me a name with about as much distinction as a grain of sand. Tighe became my middle name.

Other Smith fathers gave their children distinction. An Oklahoma man baptized his son Loyal Lodge No. 296 Knights of Pythias Ponca City Oklahoma Smith. And in Chicago there's a guy named Void Smith. My favorite real person is 5-8 Smith, who lives in Pearson, Ga.

In the navy I once received orders to become the second in command of a cruiser. I was 19 at the time. Yeah, it was another Robert Smith, who was 47 and had 23 years of service.

For years, before he died, I was always mistaken for Robert W. Smith, the publisher of the *Minneapolis Tribune* and *The Minneapolis Star*. He, of course, was mistaken for me. He always claimed that my mail was more interesting.

One of his favorite lines was that he not only opened my mail, and read it, but that he also answered it.

There are very few advantages to being a Smith. One, however, is registering at motels and hotels. You are always kidded by friends who wonder how you get away with signing into motels and hotels as Smith. Oddly enough, there never is a problem for us. One hotel clerk put it nicely: "If you were to make up a name to get into a hotel, you would use more imagination." I think that was a compliment.

This all came up because there's a new publication out titled *The Book of Smiths*, by Elsdon C. Smith. He says he worked on it for 50 years, and claims, "Almost everyone has a strain of Smith in his (or her) veins."

How did there get to be so many of us? Elsdon reports that, early on, we made the plowshares and, in wars, made the swords. In war or peace, we were important to the economy.

I suppose the author had to remind us that we Smiths never produced a president of the United States. But we did turn out a singer named Kate and a New York governor, who ran for president, named Al, and a football player named Bubba. We also did all right with a woman named Pocahontas.

Perhaps most hurtful of all is a quote from a work of Somerset Maugham: "Life must be quite different to a man called Smith; it can have neither poetry, nor distinction." What does he mean no poetry? Smith rhymes with pith, which the dictionary says is "the central cylinder of parenchymatous tissue in the stems of dictyledonous plants." Doesn't that move you a little?

Smiths, incidentally, have their own inner snobbery. We Roberts look down on all the John Smiths. And there is nothing but contempt for those who try to hide under such names as Smyth, Smythe, Smithe and the like.

That's about it. Signed: R. Tighe Smith.

A. J. — he ministers a bus

It was rush hour on a recent Friday night. The MTC bus was eastbound on Lake St. near 27th Av. S. For some reason a blind girl missed her stop. She lucked out though: She was on A. J.'s bus.

A. J. heard about the problem a few blocks later. He said to the blind girl: "That's too bad. We'll have to do something about that. Were you anxious to get home?"

"Yes," said the blind girl.

A. J. horned down a westbound bus. Then he stopped his bus, took the girl's arm and escorted her from the bus and put her on the westbound bus. No second charge for the ride.

Although it was rush hour, no one on his bus grumbled about the delay. "Everybody was smiling," said A. J.

One passenger, William Greer, was impressed. "I appreciated the very kind way he solved the problem for her," said Greer. "I'm glad to be able to tell someone about it."

Greer, a former assistant city editor of The Minneapolis Star, was not a regular customer of A. J.'s. Had he been, he would have realized that helping the blind girl was routine.

I have taken shots at rude, unthinking bus drivers. It's only fair to tell about A. J.

The Rev. A. J. Harrell, 49, has been a city bus driver for about 18 months. He is an associate minister of St. John's Baptist Church in north Minneapolis. But he doesn't get paid for that, so he supports his family by driving a bus.

His idea of bus driving is not the same as some others. He believes that when a person is running to catch his bus, the driver should stop and wait. He believes that an elderly person sometimes needs a hand in getting on a bus and getting off.

And that a shaky elderly person should be seated on the bus before it starts up. When there's no room for an elderly person to sit, A. J. asks a young person to stand. "It's funny, but they always do," he said.

A. J. thinks it is ridiculous to stop next to a huge snowdrift for disembarking passengers to fall into. Even if the snowdrift is where the normal stop is, A. J. finds a place where people can reach the sidewalk.

"I'm a minister and I just like to help people," he said. "You take the blind. I like to be the eyes for those who cannot see."

A. J. admits that not all bus drivers are like him. He gets a bit upset when he blows his horn at another bus (a signal that someone on his bus wants to transfer), and the other bus just takes off.

"But there are a lot of good bus drivers," said A. J.

On one occasion, another blind girl, who had a speech impediment, was on A. J.'s bus. She told a passenger where she wanted to get off. The passenger told A. J.

"We're a couple of blocks beyond that street," said A. J., who already was slowing down.

He stopped his bus, and said to his passengers: "Be patient, folks." Then he walked the girl back to her destination. The folks were patient.

"If I'm late, I'm late," said A. J. So far, his supervisors, who have received many compliments about him, haven't worried much about him being late.

Jerome Hines: his voice is on the bums

Two drunks were sitting in the Salvation Army building in New York's Bowery. A tall man, 6 feet 7, had talked to them and the rest of the group for awhile, and then he sang.

After it was over, one of the derelicts turned to the other and asked: "How did you like it?"

His companion said: "The tall guy talks pretty good, but he could leave out the singing."

What they didn't know is that, for nothing, they were being sung to by a man described by the *New York Times* as a singer whose "noble voice equips him for great roles, a voice certainly one of the best to be heard in opera anywhere."

The drunks had heard Jerome Hines, internationally famous opera star, a man who is approaching the record for the most seasons with the Metropolitan Opera.

And he's a man who enjoys a story like that of the two drunks.

Hines, 57, a basso who often has portrayed the devil in *Faust,* has sung free in a lot of this nation's Skid Rows and slums. But he didn't used to.

Before 1953, Hines, who will sing with the Met in Minneapolis this week, was a bit of a heller. He found solace in the things of man and had no time for the things of God. He probably wasn't any worse than the rest of us, but he was trying to be.

Traveling with the opera, in the midst of such make-believe, can be a tempting life for a tall, handsome young man. At least, Hines found it that way.

And then he found God. "It wasn't one of those quick conversions—you go to a religious meeting, hear a person speak and then you suddenly dedicate your life to God," said Hines in a telephone interview.

For a long time, he had been uneasy about his life, not satisfied with its human pleasures. And he had decided, for reasons having nothing to do with religion, to write an opera on the life of Christ. To do it, he had to read the New Testament.

Gradually, and alone, he was converted. "I decided there is a God who knows me by name," said Hines. "God is now running my show."

For a year Hines kept his conversion a secret. "I just wandered around and didn't know how to share it." Then he told people, and began his Christian life.

Hines decided to go into Skid Rows and see what he might accomplish. Without fanfare, he went to Salvation Army establishments and missions. He did whatever seemed natural, including trying to get people jobs, singing whenever appropriate, or just talking to the lonely.

"I'm not the type who goes into the streets and taps people on the shoulder and asks: 'Brother, have you been saved?'" said Hines. "I'm not saying that cannot be effective. It's just not me."

Hines is in his 33rd season with the Met. That's longer than anyone currently with the opera company. He has been signed for two more years, and if all goes well he will have 35 seasons, one more than the record of most seasons period.

He will be in Minneapolis this week to perform the role of the Marquis in Poulenc's *Dialogues of the Carmelites*. That opera will be presented Saturday night in Northrop Auditorium. Tickets are available.

Hines is not looking for credit for his work in Skid Rows, including here in the Twin Cities. But there are moments such as the time he was in the lobby of a Pittsburgh hotel.

A well-dressed man, who turned out to be a successful physician, came up to Hines and said: "I heard you sing once."

"In New York?" asked Hines. The doctor said yes.

"At the Met?" asked Hines.

"No," said the doctor. "In the Bowery. I was one of the drunks."

The doctor thanked Hines, and shook his hand. As he walked away, the doctor was crying.

May 16, 1979

ROBERT T SMITH

10 or 20 little orange things

The first graders of Hoover Elementary School in Coon Rapids have watched their mothers cook for some time now. So, as a Mother's Day project, they put together a recipe book based on their observations.

Their teacher, Sue Kaiser, did no editing whatsoever. Which was a marvelous move on her part. The prologue of the Mother's Day gift reads:

To my mom, my favorite cook, we put together this little book. I tried so hard to try and recall all the ingredients and all the amounts.

My favorite you'll find on the following pages. We hope it will be a good addition to all the cookbooks in the kitchen. I love you, mom.

The book contains 25 recipes, none of which are recommended, some of which might kill you if you tried them.

But it's a book that undoubtedly lengthened the lives of 25 mothers, if humor can do such a thing.

Jeff Ringel's recipe for chicken calls for 8 quarts of Shake 'n' Bake, 10 quarts of milk and two quarts of pepper. You bake it "until we get home from church." There is nothing in the recipe about when you begin baking it.

Another chicken recipe, from Terry Bergstrom, is unique. It follows in its entirety:

2 eggs, 1 tsp. powder, 1 spoonful sugar. But no chicken.

The cooking instructions:

Put the eggs in bowl, put powder in bowl, sugar in bowl. Cook it in the stove at one speed for 2 seconds.

Scott Conwell has a winner for spaghetti. It serves five, and contains only 100 noodles and a quarter cup of sauce. I particularly liked his instructions, obviously taken from his mother's urging, after the dish is served. To wit: **Sit up straight.**

For those who ever have made chocolate chip cookies, Phillip Schmidt's recipe should be enlightening. It calls for 40 chips and a half cup of sugar. It makes "about one or two cookies."

The instructions: **First you make dough.** That should be fun with just chips and sugar. **Make a ball. Put into stove at 200 degrees (not fahrenheit.)** Let's see, 200 degrees for you with celsius stoves would be about 392 degrees.

Here's a possible underdone pie by Lisa Kelly:

4 doughs, 1 cup frosting, 1 pie pan. Mix together. Cook it at 3 degrees for 2 hours. I assume that mix together includes the pan?

Julie Sterger, who loves her mother's meatloaf, and has watched her make it many times, came up with half an onion, a half cup of ketchup and one whole cracker. No meat. It serves eight, she said.

Not everyone was far off base. Amy Rogato, for instance, had a reasonable idea of shortcakes. You take one cake, 10 strawberries and a spoonful of whipped cream. That sounds plausible.

But I guess my favorite came from little Chad Brastad, who cannot be bothered with details. He will undoubtedly someday be a big businessman or an editor or something. His recipe for hamburgers:

1 square meat. 10 or 20 white things. 10 or 20 little orange things.

May 20, 1979

The end of the downtown characters

There was a small memorial "service" the other day for Doc Corbin. Just a few guys in the Little Wagon saloon in Minneapolis.

It's 10 years since Doc died at 91 and he held a particular distinction: he never worked a day in his life. Unless you call being a con man work.

He was maybe one of the last of the Minneapolis downtown characters. I don't know why there doesn't seem to be any characters anymore. They seem to have disappeared about the time the IDS Building was dedicated.

There was The Yeller, a fellow, harmless enough, who walked through downtown screaming some gibberish. Everyone downtown knew The Yeller, and he was tolerated.

Perhaps, today, he would be arrested and put away somewhere.

And there was The Tooth Fairy. He had specially-built false teeth and used to con restaurants. He would order something like a hard role and then, when folks were watching, he would bite into it. Voila, his teeth would clatter onto the table.

The usual settlement was about $50.

But the king of them all was Doc. He was tall, dapper and resembled a British colonel. He fancied a cane, and had a voice that Orson Welles would envy.

Doc, whose first name was Ernest, made his living basically off strangers. He would sit at a bar until what he called one of the "celophane-wrapped" suckers would appear.

"Well, young man, I'm Doc Corbin and I would like you to know that I just got in from Sioux Falls." Or Duluth or St. Louis or whatever appealed to him on a given day.

Doc would immediately buy the stranger a drink. The smart strangers, of which there seemed to be few, would offer later to buy a drink in return, and stick to that offer.

The British colonel, however, would suggest a bit of a wager.

"How about we flip for it?" he would suggest.

Now, the stranger really has nothing to lose, right? He was willing to pay for that round anyway.

So he says OK, and Doc knows the stranger is a gambler, at least of minor force. About an hour later, the stranger has lost all his money and taps Doc for cab fare.

Doc always gave the cab fare, and the stranger leaves thinking that Doc is a swell guy.

Old John Barleycorn sometimes was Doc's enemy. He'd drink too much and get a bit rattled in his gambling.

Take the time he was shooting crap behind Duff's Bar. He had his two loaded dice palmed, but when it came his turn he threw out the legitimate dice—along with his special ones. Doc could run fast.

Once in a Chicago hotel, some high rollers changed dice color to keep anyone from cheating. While they were on the green dice, Doc threw out red ones. Spent a couple days in a hospital.

But Doc wasn't all bad. He had scrupples: he never cheated the poor or widows or kids. He loved kids and would give them money whenever they needed it. Or when they didn't.

"If there was a carnival and 10,000 kids were there and Doc had $10,000, he'd give each kid a dollar," said Tony Herbert, a friendly bartender.

They say Doc made a lot of money in his lifetime. Spent a fortune on booze, they say.

But he died a pauper. I was there when they went through his belongings in his small apartment near Loring Park. There were some well-tailored suits, some other clothing and a trunk full of marked cards and loaded dice.

His landlady attended the funeral, along with The Yeller and The Tooth Fairy and someone called Short Arms.

Not unkindly, the landlady remembered: "When I'd get mad at Doc, he couldn't hear a thing. But crinkle a five-dollar bill a block away and it nearly deafened him."

At the memorial service the other day, there was a toast to Doc, not for his lifestyle, but because he was probably the end of the downtown characters. And we missed them.

May 23, 1979

For a little boy: nothing impossible

The other day I walked our son Bryan to school. It's about seven blocks from our home, but always before we drove.

Bryan goes to a Montessori School in St. Mary's Greek Orthodox Church. That's the church with the gold dome near Lake Calhoun. When you walk you can see that gold dome from blocks away. When you drive, you can't.

The reason we walked is not because I was being patriotic, and had an urge to save gasoline. It was because my car quit. The fuel pump ceased pumping, they tell

June 6, 1979

me, and I hadn't had a chance to get it fixed.

Bryan, who is 3, was delighted at the adventure. I began in a grumbling state. After all, America owes us four wheels and a functioning fuel pump. I know that if all of us walked to places, General Motors would collapse.

And, you all remember, what's good for General Motors is good for America. We know that because the chairman of the board at that time (Charlie Wilson) told us so.

Well, it was a beautiful morning. The first that happened is Bryan took hold of my hand. We cannot hold hands in a car. That would be dangerous, because one should have both hands free to steer.

Then Bryan decided that we should run a bit. "I need my exercise," he said. He had heard me say that a lot. And, as active as he is, he needs his exercise about as much as Standard Oil needs money.

After running about a block, it was time to explore. We came upon a huge motorcycle parked on the sidewalk. It was one of those machines à la the movie *Easy Rider*, and it glistened in the sun.

"Vrooooom, vrooooom." Bryan made the noises. He wanted to sit on the seat, and I didn't think the owner would mind.

A little farther, a small girl was playing in her front yard. She had a long blond ponytail and eyes with large, round circles of black ink.

"My Dad and I are walking to school," Bryan told the girl with pride in his eyes.

The girl was not impressed. Maybe she walked more than we did. In any case, she waved her hand, as a queen might who wanted to be alone. We were dismissed.

Then there were the ants. Bryan is fascinated by ants. Perhaps it's because he's closer to them than we adults. He wanted to know where they were going, what they were doing and why they don't talk.

Those are questions I could not answer.

Bryan examined a leaf-infested entrance to a storm sewer, and asked what was down below it. I told him that, when it rains, the water needs somewhere to go. And that's why we have sewers.

He asked if we could go down and see the rain water, and I told him it would be impossible. He gave me the look of a little boy for whom nothing is impossible. I remembered when I believed that, too.

Bryan stopped to look at some flowers, examined a loose dog, said hello to a mailman and watched some men blacktopping a street. Bryan asked one of the men what he was doing, and the man told him. That same man undoubtedly would not have told an adult.

As we neared the school, we saw an orange bus parked by the curb. It was empty, but the door was open and the driver was standing outside smoking. Bryan asked if he could go into the bus and the man said OK.

It was the first time Bryan had been in a school bus. He ran up and down the aisle, pinching seats and laughing. One of the first things he called by name was a school bus. He has a toy one.

It took us about a half hour to walk to his school. It takes no more than five minutes to drive. When Bryan arrived, he ran up to another little boy and said:

"Do you know what? We walked to school!"

I walked home alone. As I neared our house, I saw my car sitting impotent by the boulevard. It looked tired.

Guess I'll have to get it fixed.

June 6, 1979

The Little Wagon— a third place

They say everyone needs a third place, a place besides home and work. For me, that place is The Little Wagon.

It's one of the last downtown Minneapolis neighborhood restaurants, located at 5th Ave. S. and 4th St. Like "Cheers," it's a place "where everybody knows your name."

I have mentioned The Wagon before, in connection, for instance, with The Better Than Nothing Dirt Band that plays at my third place on Tuesday nights. I play trumpet.

The Wagon needs fuller explanation. It is frequented by newspaper people, grain

ROBERT T SMITH

November 7, 1979

brokers and city hall politicians. You seldom see a stranger there.

We go to weddings, bar mitzvahs and funerals of customers of The Wagon. In a sense, it's more European than American. It's a place where people live, not just a place to eat and drink.

The late Pete the Printer held forth there for decades. He was known for his puns. Celebrities come in occasionally and like the place because nobody hassles them for autographs and such. A local chimney sweep, black top hat and sooty face, gets no silly questions.

I remember Old Annie, a waitress in her 80s, who was very literal minded. I had to drive to Bemidji one time and I knew Old Annie grew up there. So, I asked her what was the best way to drive to her home town.

"Either by bus or by car," was her only reply. OK.

Not long ago, a young waitress was about to have her first baby. Her husband had abandoned her, and funds were low. The Wagon people came up with $400 and gifts for the baby.

Former owner Bob Sorenson was an easy touch. Once, Columnist Larry Batson had to take a British visitor to a rather fancy restaurant. He discovered he had left his billfold at home.

He went to Bob to borrow $30 to spend in another cafe.

Sorenson gave him $50, saying: "At that place, you'll need it." When he retired, Bob left a drawer-full of I.O.U.s that never were collected.

Some strange things have happened in The Wagon. A young man came in one morning and proceeded to take off all his clothes and stand near the front door.

Two elderly women were having breakfast in a booth not 10 feet from the man. Police were called and the man was hustled to jail.

The waitress came to the women and apologized for what she thought must have been a harrowing experience.

"Oh," said one of the ladies, "we thought he was a statue."

A prominent financial consultant liked the place so much that, when he found the woman of his choice, he got married there. Minister, Dirt Band and all.

I guess my favorite story involves a holdup man. He came in one day with a gun and a note telling Sorenson to put money in a bag.

Just then, the late Halsey Hall, dean of sports writers and announcers, came in. He bumped into the holdup man and said to Sorenson: "My man, how are you today?"

"Just fine, Halsey," said Sorenson, lying.

"Are you Halsey Hall?" asked the holdup man.

"Yes, my man," said Halsey.

The holdup man dropped everything and left. Why? I'd guess he decided he didn't want to rob Halsey's place.

Or maybe he sensed that The Little Wagon is a community affair, not to be violated.

November 7, 1979

She died after returning from Oz

As Judy herself put it, "For such a mixed-up life later, it started out beautifully." She remembered Grand Rapids as all charm and gaiety, a lovely town of little white houses surrounded by blue lakes, and tiny ponds, the corner house she lived in with a truck garden in back and corn growing wild between the sidewalk and the curb in front, the snow all about—it started snowing in September—and ice skating, with hot green mint tea to drink afterward.

From "Judy," by Gerold Frank

Grand Rapids, Minn.

Judy Garland was the first woman ever that I loved. I was about 16 and learned later she was older than I, but it didn't seem that way at the time.

It wasn't just because she wowed me with her voice, her "Over the Rainbow" and her singing "You Made Me Love You" to a picture of Clark Gable. (I never liked Clark Gable much.)

About a week ago, I was in Grand Rapids. I decided to indulge in some nostalgia, actually some sentimentality. I

November 7, 1979   ROBERT T SMITH

walked around Grand Rapids, thinking of Judy, and agreed it was *a lovely town of little white houses, surrounded by blue lakes.*

Until she was about 5, Judy lived in a two-story white house at 727 NE 2nd Av. The house, with a front porch, is still there.

I stood across the street from the Rialto Theater on the main drag. When Judy was in Grand Rapids in the 1920s, the town's theater was called the New Grand, and it was run by her father, Frank Gumm.

There is some controversy over whether the Grand was in the same location as the Rialto, but all seem to agree it was in the same block.

It was at the New Grand, at age 2, that Judy, then known as Baby Gumm, made her debut. Her father had inaugurated an amateur night at the theater and Judy, a tiny person as an adult, got up and sang, "My Country 'Tis of Thee." Reports her biographer, Gerold Frank: "Baby sang every word, sustaining the tune to the end, her voice clear and pure, and surprisingly strong for so small a child."

In 1938, while she was making "The Wizard of Oz," Judy came to Grand Rapids and appeared at the old theater for the local folks.

Part of the old Central Grade School, in the heart of town, is devoted to a Garland museum. It was instigated by Jackie Dingmann, an artist, who decided that Judy's birthplace needed something to honor her.

Recently, when Judy's daughter, Liza Minnelli, was in Minneapolis, Dingmann visited her. "She was marvelous, and said she wanted some day to come to Grand Rapids to see where her mother was born."

I remembered the time I met Judy in New York City. It was after *Oz* and the Andy Hardy movies and the musical comedies with Mickey Rooney. Long after.

She was having trouble with booze and drugs and weight and husbands. I was working for *Time* magazine and they wanted me to find her, to find out what happened to little Dorothy.

We met in a second-rate hotel in Manhattan. She was disheveled and anxious and distant. But I remember one thing she said to me: "Put down in your notebook that Judy Garland never learned how to love. I grew up a little in your state, Grand Rapids. But I never learned to love my parents.

"And then I went to that zoo, that MGM lot in Hollywood. And I certainly never learned to love there. And then I was married. I can't remember now, four times, five times . . . And I never learned to love my husbands."

It was not long after that, she had her triumphant success in the likes of Carnegie Hall. And then, in 1969, at age 47, she was found dead of an overdose in a London Hotel.

I thought about all that as I wandered around Grand Rapids, a most pleasant community that no longer has corn growing wild between the sidewalks and the curbs.

I wondered what would have happened to Judy Garland had she remained in this town.

Then I decided that my first love never lived to be 47. She died shortly after returning from Oz.

ROBERT T SMITH   November 11, 1979

"I wear shoes made of mountains"

Did you ever hear of wind tigers?
They fly!
They whistle because the air

goes right through them.
They have holes.
They fly into the windows of
imagination.

That poem is one of the results of the efforts of 50,000 people in Minnesota. It was written by Debby O'Brien of St. Anthony. She's a fifth grader in Silver Oak Elementary School.

Debby's poem is included in *An Explosion of White Petals,* a publication of the Minnesota Poets in the Schools project.

That project involves 50,000 people, including students, teachers, professional poets and interested community members. Poets in the Schools is one of the efforts of Community Programs in the Arts and Sciences (COMPAS), an agency of the St. Paul-Ramsey Arts and Science Council.

To steal one of Debby's lines, Poets in the Schools is designed to let children "fly into the windows of imagination." And, believe me, they do.

Consider this from Jill Miller, a third-grader at Washburn Elementary in Bloomington:

On the day of the eclipse
in mid-afternoon
I listen for feathers.
I search for dreams.
I climb the sky.
I watch for rivers of silver.
I am lost among treetops.
I begin with Z.
I wear shoes made of mountains
and I sleep through darkness
with teachers at my feet.

To read *White Petals* is to realize there are many Minnesota children, urban and rural, with spirit and imagination and, in some cases, deep troubles.

Mark Vinz, a teacher and writer who edited the publication, put it this way:

"I've tried to emphasize both variety and surprise. The predominant theme in the poems is intensely personal feeling, often painful, almost always frank.

"This reaffirms for me some of the basic principles of all poetry: to discover and express parts of us that are hidden (sometimes from ourselves), to reach out, to learn how to find new words, new ways of perceiving both the inner and outer worlds."

Andrea McAllister, a 12th-grader at Battle Lake High School, offers one of those intensely personal poems:

Hot, dry eyed
I grab my coat and slam the door.
Dusk around me, nearly night.
I look at the bare trees
silhouetted against the sky.
Dry leaves scurry around my feet
as if in a frenzy to get nowhere—
sort of like me.

Another personal offering I like is from Chris James, an 11th-grader at Mariner High School, White Bear Lake. It deals with his frustrations of being an adolescent:

It so happens I am sick of being
me
I can't go to R rated movies
Can't get good jobs
I have to obey my parents
I have a curfew . . .
Can't become a U. S. Senator
Can't write good poems
My feet are too big
I can't write neatly
I can't

Lest you think that all the poems are intense, be assured there is humor among the state's young. Richard Devick, fifth-grader at Our Lady of the Lake Elementary in Mound broke me up with his "Last Will and Testament." In part:

I leave $5,000,000,000,000,000 that you
will find
in my Piggy Bank . . . Send it to Heaven.
And give my underwear to my sister.
Don't forget . . .

December 23, 1979

ROBERT T SMITH

And give my leftover sandwich (half eaten)
    to Sandra, my dog.
I give my bad dream about killer bees to
    my sister . . .
I leave my fleet of ships that cost more
    than
$1,000,000 to my brother. I leave my
    money which
even computers can't count to my Uncle
    Mark.
I also leave South America to my sister.

The children whose poems are in the publication will give a reading at noon Saturday in the Landmark Center, 75 W. 5th St., St. Paul.

The poems I selected in this column are not necessarily the best. I don't know which are the best.

I just know that *White Petals* fascinates me. Where else could you read of wearing "shoes made of mountains?"

December 23, 1979

Christmas: think of love, not presents

A note to our son, Bryan, 4, the one who loved the tree:

Last year, you were too young to pay much attention to Christmas. You were much more fascinated with the lights and the multicolored wrapping paper than with such things as presents.

But now you're more grown up. You know what a toy is. You get very excited over a gift no matter what it is. You say "Wow!" even over the cheapest of things. You are not spoiled. Not yet. . . .

We are not going to buy you much for Christmas, Bryan. We feel that, for us, the emphasis should be different.

That doesn't mean, Bryan, that you won't get some Christmas presents. There's no way to stop your grandparents from buying you something, although we have stopped them from buying us anything.

But you won't get a lot of things. I know this year it won't matter that much to you. But we want to start early and condition you for other years, too.

We want all your Christmases to be a time when you think of love and joy and get an inner feeling of warmth. We do not want your Christmases to be a time to think of how much you will get.

In the future, you may be subjected to the peer pressure we felt when we were young. The question asked of many of our little friends: "What did you get for Christmas?" And those who asked were usually those who got a lot for Christmas.

I remember one Christmas, during the Depression, when my parents had very little money. I got one present. It was a little truck that cost 89 cents. I was thrilled, because I didn't know it wasn't expensive.

On Christmas day, a little girl who lived down the block asked me what I got. I told her with great pride.

"Is that all?" she said. Then she recited the list of what she received.

A small boy can be jealous. I went home and told my mother what the little girl had said.

My mother wasn't the most educated person in the world. And it's unfortunate for you, Bryan, that she died before you were born. For my mother had her own kind of wisdom. She picked me up and nestled me in her lap.

"You got all we could give you," she said. "I'll bet that little girl's parents could have given her even more than she got."

I was too young to get all the meaning of that. But I got enough. . . .

So, I guess what we're trying to say, Bryan, is that we hope that you'll never get a lot of presents for Christmas. We hope that you grow up to look forward to Christmas without a sense of greed.

Your mother has a great idea which we will initiate this Christmas. Janet has suggested that she and your older sister, Amy, and I each have one night before Christmas during which we will read something aloud, or create something. The idea is that whatever we say will be meaningful and thus help us understand one another. You will be present at these sessions even though you won't understand. But in future years . . .

We want you to think of Santa Claus

ROBERT T SMITH — May 9, 1980

without the bag of toys on his back. We would prefer that you looked upon him as a spirit who delivers trust rather than toy soldiers, who dispenses love rather than licorice.

We hope, Bryan, that you never grow too sophisticated to say "Wow!" at an 89-cent truck or become too worldly to not be thrilled by a sparrow in the winter, or to love a tree.

And, if some day some little friend asks you what you got for Christmas, we hope you'll say: "All my parents could give."

Neville Marriner, music director of the Minnesota Orchestra, conducted the Better Than Nothing Dirt Band at a downtown saloon. Band members were Skip Heine, trombone (slide visible at left); Dan Byrne, guitar; Bob Evans, concertina; Phil Schrader, harmonica; Roger Budde, banjo; Dick Caldwell, drums; Jim Fuller, bass; Bob Watson, clarinet; professional musician Red Wolfe, Robert T. Smith, trumpet. The banners read, "Last night 'The Creation.' Tonight: Armageddon!"

May 9, 1980

Marriner: a pearl before swine

The Better Than Nothing Dirt Band, which can empty a room quicker than an agitated skunk, had a guest conductor Thursday night: Neville Marriner, music director of the Minnesota Orchestra.

Why such an accomplished musician would enter The Little Wagon, a saloon at 4th St. and 5th Av. S., and conduct such a band is explained by the maestro himself:

"This is just what I needed. An opportunity to sample more of life in Minneapolis. And I can deal with great musicians anytime..."

Marriner is not your stuffy symphony conductor. He had a ball.

When he arrived with his wife, Molly, who insisted on coming, he was presented with a baton.

With an elfish smile, he said: "For this group, I do not need a baton. A straw will do."

The packed house laughed and he had them from there on.

Wednesday night, Marriner, in white tie and tails, conducted Haydn's oratorio, "The Creation."

At the Little Wagon, Marriner, wearing a tan sport coat and white turtleneck, was greeted with foot-high letters reading: "Last night: 'The Creation.' Tonight: Armageddon!"

Slipping in with the atmosphere as easily as donning a silk dinner jacket, Marriner asked at one point if the band would play Beethoven's Fifth.

"Hum a few bars and we'll fake it," said the concertina player.

Marriner broke up. The band played the first famous four notes of the Fifth and then went into "My Wild Irish Rose." Marriner cheered.

"All I can say," he said, "is your Fifth is more like a Second."

Waving the baton we gave him, Marriner played the game beautifully, with humor and grace. He tried to coax notes where they didn't exist. He tried to stop us, to no avail.

We told our guest conductor that our major fear is that, if we practice too diligently, we might one day lose our identity as the world's worst band and become mediocre.

"Don't worry," said Marriner.

For his visit, the Britisher was presented with the First Annual Little Wagon Award for Valor. He got the framed certificate for:

"Having demonstrated consummate courage in entering The Little Wagon, in her majesty's former colony, and subsequently having consorted with The Better Than Nothing Dirt Band...

"It is acknowledged that no other artist has so openly and willingly risked career and reputation for so miniscule a cause. Ars gratia artis."

It all started when we heard that Marriner, unlike some symphony types, was a spontaneous fellow who liked off-beat experiences. What could be more off-beat? we reasoned. And we were right.

For instance, Mariner once said that one of the two people he most wanted to meet was Goldie Hawn. Our kind of guy.

We also read about the wonderful music he has made in the basement of St. Martin-in-the-Fields, one of London's historic churches. It was a place for tramps and dropouts and drinkers and drug addicts.

Reminisced Marriner earlier: "Once someone came in and pulled a knife on the curate, who said, 'Don't be silly,' and took the weapon away from him. And I remember a fight between a couple of drunks during the B minor Mass over a seat—probably the place that one of them usually slept in."

We figured he'd feel right at home in the Wagon. Our kind of guy:

And then there was the time the trim, sandy-haired conductor said, in 1956, that the London Symphony Orchestra "was the worst orchestra in London by far, absolutely the worst."

That's a title we long have claimed, so we thought we'd show him what worst really is.

Thus Marriner received an invitation from the band members. As he has on other occasions, Red Wolfe, a real professional trumpeter, dropped in last night.

Outside of Wolfe, all the band members work at jobs other than music. It has something to do with eating regularly.

After hearing us play a few tunes with Red, Marriner approached him and asked, in his British accent: "How did you get caught up in all this?"

The 55-year-old Marriner, known for his candor and irreverent wit, was born in Lincoln, England. He plays a violin when he's not up front. However, he had the good sense not to bring his instrument near us.

He mumbled something about a pearl before swine.

But actually he was charming. He had a beer and talked about why he came. "There's nothing worse to unwind in than a quiet restaurant. I need to let off steam, and this is the place. I'd come back here just to listen."

Shortly before he left I announced to the crowd that, since we invited him to our place, we assumed that he would invite us to Orchestra Hall. The audience laughed so loudly I didn't hear what he said.

As he and Molly left, we played "Colonel Bogie's March," that great British tune.

July 28, 1980

A couch is his fire truck

What happens to a child's imagination? Where does it go when we grow up and become that ugly word: adult?

I suspect all too often it is trampled by much-less important forces in life. We get involved with that silliness called reality. There's an old saying I'd like to change a bit: adults may dream of castles in the sky. Children live in them.

Son Bryan, 4, is currently a fire chief, a pirate captain, a driver of trains, a seeker of whales. I am only a newspaper columnist.

No, wait. I am also a fire chief's assistant, an ordinary pirate, a lowly railroad employee and a boat rower for a seeker of whales.

Bryan began creating the games about two months ago. It doesn't take much to make him plunge into a role. A cheap red fireman's helmet. A balloon with a skull and crossbones on it.

It all occurs in one room of the house—an enclosed front porch made up almost entirely of windows.

Outside the windows is the sea, or Moby Dick or a railroad track or a burning hotel.

Bryan, aside from being the creator of the games, is also the producer, director and propman.

He finds the props himself. A broom handle is his harpoon. A long couch is his fire truck. He unscrewed two legs of a

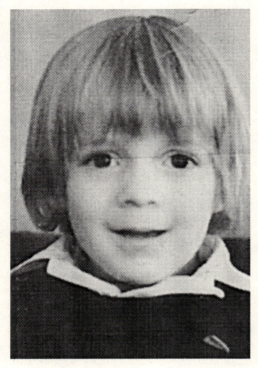

small yellow plastic chair. They are hollow and make excellent pirate telescopes. Turn the chair on its side, and the remaining two legs are cannon.

He steers the ship with an 8 mm. film reel. His whale boat is a large davenport cushion. I row it with mop handles. When we fight a fire, I am the ladder.

There is a script for each game. Bryan makes that up, too.

When we play railroad, for instance, I must stay in another room while Bryan sets up the porch train. Then, on signal, I arrive—late.

"You're late," says the driver of trains.

"Sorry, chief, I overslept," I say.

"Been doing that a lot lately," says Bryan.

(I must report that, in his various roles, his voice changes. As a driver of trains, he lowers it and is very serious. As a pirate captain, he is more bold and blustery. His voice is loud and often harsh. As a seeker of whales, he whispers—so as not to scare away his quarry.)

But back to train. On the bottom of a paper plate, Bryan has drawn the map of our route. I might conclude that it is just a bunch of intersecting lines that mean nothing.

Years ago, I would have noticed right away it was a map.

The scripts do not change much. He creates new games, but he insists that once he has perfected them they must be played the same each time.

"Where are we going today, chief?" I always ask.

Bryan carefully scrutinizes the "map," and then comes up with a place. One day he said: "Hawaii."

I thought I had him.

"Hawaii is across the ocean," I said.

"The train can go on water," he said.

Years ago I would have known that.

It should be pointed out that, in playing pirate, we are good guys. I questioned him about this once, and he informed me that we were sort of like Robin Hoods.

"And we don't kill people," he said, "we just shoot at them."

I contribute almost nothing. Once, I suggested that we go to Miami on the train. It was a very cold day.

Well, you see, I didn't know that a large section of the train track to Miami had been torn up by a tornado. Years ago, I would have known that.

On this day, we went to the North Pole.

"Are there train tracks all the way to the North Pole?" I asked.

"Just finished the last mile yesterday," said Bryan, giving me the look of one who is beginning to wonder about my ignorance.

Years ago, I would have known about the tracks to the North Pole.

October 27, 1980   ROBERT T SMITH

Her commitment is infectious

Beth Puncochar plays Euchre with an elderly man who is disoriented, but who loves the card game. She patiently talks

and reads poetry to an elderly woman who cannot speak.

Another elderly woman, who declines to speak to everyone else, will talk to Beth.

Beth dances with elderly men, and helps those with hearing and vision problems to play bingo or bunco. These are just some of the things Beth does for the residents of Mala Strana, a nursing home in New Prague, Minn.

So, Beth is a middle-aged woman whose children have left home and who has time on her hands?

No, she is 13, and has put in hundreds of hours of volunteer work at Mala Strana since she was 6.

For her efforts, Beth has been named 1980 national Teen Volunteer of the Year by the American Health Care Association. There's just one named each year to that title. She will be honored at the Minnesota Association of Health Care Facilities convention Nov. 19 in the Radisson South Hotel. There also will be a reception for her Dec. 7 at Mala Strana.

Beth, an eighth-grader at New Prague Junior High School, doesn't know what the fuss is all about. She doesn't consider herself a do-gooder or a helper of mankind.

"I just like old people," she said. "It's fun to do things for them."

When she was a first grader, Beth went to Mala Strana one day with a neighbor. She immediately started helping—and that was before the nursing home had a volunteer program.

In nominating Beth for the national award, Jacki Kes, Mala Strana volunteer coordinator, wrote:

One of Beth's unique qualities is that she prefers to visit the residents who have the greatest need for social interaction and special help . . .

Beth does, indeed, enrich and enhance the lives of the residents at Mala Strana. It is refreshing to have her within our midst . . .

Her volunteer work is only part of her life. She also is involved in softball, volleyball and basketball and forgoes her study hall time to work in the school office.

The enthusiastic young girl is a kind of one-man-band in terms of volunteer work. On her own, Beth has recruited other young volunteers, including her little brother, Jimmy, 10. "Her commitment is infectious," said Kes.

And on her own, she visits Mala Strana residents who are hospitalized and reports back to the other residents on how they're doing. She also does followup visits with residents who have been discharged to their homes.

It is difficult to write about Beth without feeling guilty. At 13, I played baseball and chewed bubblegum instead of helping anyone. I suspect some of you others out there did about the same.

Let's see, that's about all about Beth, I guess.

No. She regularly visits a neighbor, Dan Picha. She walks with him and takes him shopping. Picha is blind.

And she's only 13.

ROBERT T SMITH December 28, 1980

A washed out bride on the creek

The other car collided with mine without giving warning of its intention. I thought my window was down, but found it was up when I put my hand through it . . .

I first saw the slow-moving, sad-faced old gentleman when he bounced off the hood of my car.

I told the police I was not injured, but on removing my hat I found I had a fractured skull . . .

Well, Wes Dow, an old friend, is at it again. He's a former editor around these newspapers and is the world's most enthusiastic collector of trivia.

His latest interest forwarded to me involves actual statements made by motorists on insurance claim forms. Some I had seen before, but many I hadn't.

I have written before about Wes, now 85 and living in Champlin. He also was a collector of errors in newspapers. A couple I still remember:

Medford, Wis.—The petition by Oswald Conrad, chairman of the town of Criteria, called for $600 to repair a washed out bride on the Elder Creek.

Minneapolis—Mrs. Jackson, who was graduated from Vassar at the age of 20, never regained consciousness.

And there were a few actual headlines I cherish: Amputation Posts to Install Heads; Clothes to be Worn by Wedding Guests; Rabbits Being Drafted for Military Service (should have been rabbis).

But back to the insurance forms:

A truck backed through my windshield into my wife's face.

My car was legally parked when it backed into the other vehicle.

A pedestrian I did not see hit me, then went hiding under my car.

To avoid hitting the bumper of the car in front, I struck the pedestrian.

An invisible car came out of nowhere, struck my vehicle and vanished.

With his usual humor, Wes concocted his own obituary 27 years ago. Referring to himself in the third person, he wrote:

"Served in World War II as a supply sergeant for four B29 groups. Did so well, that after the war he didn't have to buy socks or underwear for 7 years and no shoes for 12. A record . . . Also never had a venereal disease."

He ended it with: "Any questions? Sorry, you're too late!"

His "funeral services" also were decreed by him:

"They will be short accompanied by martinis. Would like two myself. Would like to wear my red shirt if possible, in case anyone wants to go deer hunting afterwards . . ."

Humor to Wes always has been involved with the foibles of human nature. He likes the funny things that really happen rather than jokes. That explains his interest in the auto insurance form statements. No one could fake such statements as:

I was taking my canary to the hospital. It got loose and flew out the window. The next thing I saw was his rear end, and there was a crash.

The other guy was all over the road. I had to swerve a number of times before I hit him.

February 25, 1981   ROBERT T SMITH

The accident happened when the right front door of a car came around the corner without giving a signal.

I was sure the old fellow would never make it to the other side of the road when I struck him.

Coming home, I drove into the wrong house and collided with a tree I don't have.

Then there is my all-time favorite:

I pulled away from the side of the road, glanced at my mother-in-law and headed over the embankment.

February 25, 1981

Nell has friends with guns and clubs

There are a whole lot of cops in Minneapolis looking for two men who hurt *What-the-Hell-Nell.*

Nell Erickson, 66, has been a favorite of Minneapolis police for many years. She is their unofficial mother, known and loved by the badge wearers all over town.

Ironically, I wrote about her about seven years ago. The beginning of the column:

It was dark when two hoods approached the woman as she was about to enter her home. One knocked her down and the other was about to grab her purse when he shouted: 'My God, it's Nell, you dumbo. Let's get the hell out of here.'

It's a good thing they didn't really hurt Nell or take her money. They would have had about 600 policemen working day and night to get them.

Well, this time two hoods did hurt her . . .

In the 1970s, Nell, who often used the words *What-the-Hell* when mothering the police, ran and was part-owner of Joe Houle's Peanut Bar at 2647 Nicollet Av.

It was two doors down from the Minneapolis Police Department's Sixth Precinct. Nell has since retired, the Sixth Precinct was closed by Police Chief Anthony Bouza and the bar is under new ownership.

But, although retired, Nell kept in touch with her "babies."

Nell had worked in Lake St. area taverns since 1933, starting in a joint near the Bryant Precinct. "The Bryant cops raised me," she says. She has done everything for policemen from patching their injuries and their psyches to patching their pants.

She threw them parties on their birth-

days, anniversaries, and when the rookies were graduated to the force. Occasionally, she closed up Houle's and threw them a party for no particular reason. "Maybe the boys would have a bad week so we'd have a Bad Week Party."

No wonder they love her.

Nell also adopted city firemen on one occasion. She decided they weren't properly honored, too. So she threw the First Annual City Firemen's Appreciation Bash at Houle's.

"They risk their lives just like policemen," she said, "so why not some free old-fashioned goulash and a hug." She didn't however, really change loyalties. "The cops are still my loves," she said at the time.

The police have given to Nell, too. She has a pair of silver eagles on her blouse — the insignia of a deputy police chief. Elmer Nordlund, former chief, gave them to her. And former mayor Charles Stenvig, a policeman, gave her a Distinguished Service Award, which reads in part:

ROBERT T SMITH

"Nell has made her life by supporting the police, giving a helping hand to one who needs it, or a sympathetic ear to one in trouble."

The lady has a regulation badge that says *What-the-Hell-Nell* on it, and a full-power police radio in her home. On her 60th birthday, cops from downtown, the east side, the north side, you name it, came to honor her.

Now, Nell is in room 707B at Metropolitan Medical Center. She is crippled, and has a two-inch break in her spine. Her story, which she filed with the police:

She was walking on 26th St. between Nicollet and 1st Av. S., a while back when two men came up behind her. They asked for the address of Chief Bouza. She said she didn't know.

"You must know," one man said. "You're one of them."

Nell remained mute.

"So, they called me a pig lover and hit me in the back with brass knuckles."

Nell says she is now having to deal with crutches, a cane and a wheelchair. She has other physical problems, she said, besides the back injury, but she contends that is the most serious.

No matter, the two assailants, who said they were from New York City and who Nell thinks wanted to kill Bouza, had better be in Timbuktu by now.

"No one hurts Nell without getting us really upset," said Capt. Bruce Lindberg, head of internal affairs, former head of the Sixth Precinct and a good friend of Nell's.

There has been a succession of policemen—captains and lieutenants and sergeants and patrolmen—visiting Nell in the hospital.

"They're beautiful," she said Tuesday. "They're my lifeline."

And they owe her.

July 16, 1981

Richard Harris: "Camelot" is a dream

Where once it never rained 'til after
*   sundown:*
by 8 a.m. the morning fog had flown.
Don't let it be forgot,
that once there was a spot,
for one brief, shining moment
that was known as Camelot.

From "Camelot"

To me, he *is* King Arthur, because I don't believe King Arthur existed. I don't want him to be real.

I don't want Richard Harris to be real either.

To me, Harris, who is somewhere around 50 (take your pick from encyclopedias and such), is one of the last of the true romantics. Who else would sing at the sun while riding a bicycle while holding a basket full of seaweed?

And who else would insist on writing poetry that he says is "nothing astoundingly philosophical?"

And who else has had his nose broken seven times, sometimes in pub brawls, yet can don the attire of King Arthur and make you believe that, for one brief, shining moment, there was a magic called Camelot?

Harris can.

He was in Minneapolis Tuesday for the opening of *Camelot* at the Orpheum Theater. It will continue through Aug. 1.

Harris attended a press conference wearing a fedora, white athletic socks, running shoes and a navy-blue scarf—topped off with orange-tinted glasses.

If he was bored by all the questions, as I suspect King Arthur would have been, he hid it behind his Irish charm and wit.

What does he think of Hollywood? "I'm not into pictures anymore . . . Clint Eastwood, Charles Bronson, Robert Redford—they're the best at doing one role. And it's bankable. The public doesn't want to see them doing anything else . . . But to me they're faltering . . .

"Burt Reynolds. You put him in cars and he drives off cliffs, and there's no story. He does it better than anyone else . . . The same old breasts, different faces . . ."

How about his stormy career involving women and bar fights? "Both the same," he said. He pointed out that, at least in the past, he and Richard Burton and Peter O'Toole "lived far more extraordinary lives than the performances we gave."

Then he began a soliloquy on women's rights:

"I'm all for equality. But they may have gone a step too far. It's a crusade that may have lost sight of its goals."

He told of a plumber who telephoned a talk show on women's rights and complained that he hated having his head in toilets all day, but he had no men's rights organization to get his head out of them.

"You see the point?" asked Harris. "Women don't want to be housewives. But 80 percent of the male population are doing things they don't want to do. It all can lose balance . . ." Where did he get the 80 percent figure? You don't ask that of an Irish king.

In 1963, Harris won the Cannes Film Festival best actor award for *This Sporting Life,* a low-budget, low-key story.

Would a film like that be made today, and would it be appreciated?

Harris answered that question in several ways. He said he didn't think such a picture would be made today, but that people *would* appreciate it.

"The American people are very bright. It is the people who make policy in creating films who have no taste," he said.

He didn't understand why the most recent Tennessee Williams play lasted only about a week in New York. Low attendance, or course, killed it. But what does an Irish king know about money?

"Williams has got to have a public!" proclaimed Harris.

Harris did King Arthur in the very successful 1967 Joshua Logan movie version of the musical. And he's done it hundreds of times since.

The man, born in Limerick, Ireland, and raised in the British theater, gave the best answer to the hackneyed question of how he can do *Camelot* night after night without losing the spark.

"It's technique," he said. "We in the British theater are more aware of technique. And when I get out on that stage and play King Arthur, I believe in him."

In other words, he's a pro and a pro is expected to do his work and not expected to get bored with it. And, if he's bored with it, he depends on the technique.

Why has *Camelot* existed so long?

The tall man with the young blue eyes and long amber hair thought for a moment.

"I think it started with the Kennedy era. There was a sense of great leadership then. And there was Pope John the 23rd, who touched millions with his leadership.

"There was a whole new sense of honest, decent purpose. And they thought of 'Camelot' as a sort of national anthem.

"Now there is no such leadership. So 'Camelot' has become a dream or perhaps a prayer."

Not long from now, Harris is going to Broadway to do *Hamlet.* That appeals to him, and he feels it's now or never.

"I'm getting old. It's *Hamlet* now or, in three years, I'll have to do Polonius."

There was little doubt Harris had charmed those who were there, including some young women who shook his hand—and may not wash their hands for a month.

ROBERT T SMITH August 19, 1981

He was on his good behavior, but you wondered how soon it would be before he would again be riding that bicycle and singing at the sun.

August 19, 1981

Kara: she never asks "Why me?"

*If it weren't for you,
our lives would be less.*
             From "A Ballad for Kara"

Patrick Riley, who has been in surgery at Children's Health Center for eight years, has seen many kids with medical problems. Some have not lived. But he's written only one song.

That's "A Ballad for Kara," an Irish tune for an extraordinary girl, Kara Folsom, 8.

"She's such an alive kid," said Riley, 31, a surgical nurse. "She's got my number, I guess."

When you add up her problems, you would easily forgive her if she were a morose, angry, depressed child.

She was born with a cleft spine and her bladder on the outside. She has scoliosis

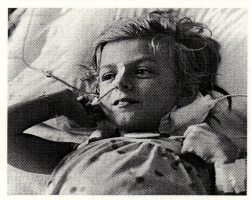

(another spine disorder), a congenital hip malformation, one club foot and the other the opposite of that.

In her young life, she has had six major operations, one in which they removed one kidney and her bladder.

Reports her mother, Beverly Folsom, 39, of Pine River, Minn.:

The doctors said she'd never crawl. So, she crawled. They said she'd never stand, so she stood. They said she certainly never would walk. So, she walks.

Kara not only walks, she is the only one in her school class who can stand on her head unaided, and she can do cartwheels.

Her mother does not take credit for any of that. "We never pushed Kara," she said. "But somewhere she got the motivation. Nobody knows where. She's just different."

There is a maturity about Kara that her mother calls "almost spooky at times." Kara, for instance, when she can, will go about the hospital "taking care" of other sick children. She's very good with them.

On the occasions when she returns to the health center at 2525 Chicago Av., the word spreads throughout the place that Kara is back. She never lacks for visits from the staff.

She loves art, and there's a crayon drawing hanging on the nearby nurses' station. On it says: "For the nurses, from Kara." She takes care of them, too.

Monday she had three tubes in her, dispensing various fluids to her frail body. She is recovering from her sixth operation.

But, in a bright blue dress and red shoes, she received Riley and others for the presentation of the ballad. By her bed was a picture of Kevin McHale, the pro basketball player from Minnesota, on whom she has a crush. Also a loud sign that says, "Send a Pizza to My Room," and balloons, lots of balloons.

For some time, Riley and other hospital employees had been wearing homemade buttons that read: "Club Member: Kara Folsom Secret Admirers."

Playing his concertina and accompanied by staffer Leslie Martin on a penny whistle, Riley started the ballad:

*Oh, say, have you heard of sweet Kara
    Folsom . . . ?*

Kara gave Riley the look of a coquette. It explained why Riley, who should be a bit used to seriously ill children, says such things as, "I'm not sure when I first fell in love with Kara."

Then Kara smiled. Her charisma told of a girl who goes to Pine River Elementary School in regular class, and who does well.

It told of a girl who is sometimes hurt a

October 12, 1981

ROBERT T SMITH

bit when other children make fun of her, but who shrugs it off—even though her mother cries all night about it.

It told of a girl with physical problems, but whose favorite subject in school is gym. And of a girl who never asks "Why me?" because it wouldn't occur to her.

She's been through it all and she's always bounced back. . . .

Kara's joy at the song filled the room. It is difficult to describe how an 8-year-old girl can seem so full of charm. You wonder if all her problems didn't help.

You have no doubts when her mother tells you that her other children—Guy, 18, Dawn, 17, Dale, 16, Lee Ann, 13—"are much better, more compassionate people because of Kara." And why grownups are so attracted to her.

A smile and your bright eyes on your face now belong,
for that is the price of my singing this song.

Kara paid the price.

And, as you might see, Kara's got my number, too.

October 12, 1981

At 87, he's still airborne

Charlie Sellman claims that flying an airplane regularly keeps him young. It must work, because he's 87 and still piloting.

Other things that tend to keep Charlie young:

He works in the fields 10 hours a day during planting and harvesting seasons.

He skis regularly during the winter.

And he rides his adult tricycle every day. In the winter he ties rope around the tires, using it as "chains" to get through snow.

Charlie contends that he's the oldest active pilot in the United States. He has been claiming that for years—at air shows around the country—and no one has challenged him yet. (There are no records concerning old pilots.)

Every other year Charlie passes an extensive physical to renew his pilot's li-

cense. The only restriction is that he must wear glasses. There is no age limit for private pilots.

His insurance company used to make him take a physical each year that he didn't have a flight physical, but they stopped doing that years ago.

Charlie has his own airport, Sellman Field, named after him. It's on a farm about 3 miles west of Mabel and includes two hangars and a 2,500-foot runway that looks like a well-kept lawn.

He maintains the airstrip himself, cutting the grass and trapping gophers.

"It's great up in the sky," Charlie said. "Downright relaxing."

Charlie was born in Iowa and started farming in the Mabel area in 1950. He did well raising beef cattle and hogs and some corn and oats.

He began flying in 1935. He saw Max Conrad, famed Winona pilot, barn-storming and decided he wanted to try it.

"I thought it was a right quick way to travel," Charlie said.

For years, Charlie did some barn-storming himself. He recalls one act that was particularly entertaining:

"One of us pilots would dress up like a lady. Then the announcer at the air show would tell the folks that the 'lady' was being taken for a plane ride. As the pilot was loading her onto the plane, he would get notice of a phone call for him.

"When he leaves, the 'lady' starts up the plane and takes off alone. The announcer goes a bit berserk and the 'lady' flies the heck out of that plane—loop-the-loops, stalls, the whole bag of tricks.

"Then allegedly she runs out of gas, and makes a dead-stick landing. Quite a show."

During his barnstorming days, he got to know Charles Lindbergh and Amelia Earhart: "They were around a lot."

Charlie bought his first plane, a single-engine Luscombe, in 1947 and flew it for 22 years. When he sold it he bought his present plane, a Piper Cherokee. Cost him $10,000 and he put in another $5,000 worth of radio and navigation equipment.

"I can fly anywhere and land anywhere with the equipment I've got," he said. "It's a dandy little plane."

ROBERT T SMITH   August 12, 1984

Charlie was 70 when he bought the Cherokee. Not everyone was thrilled with a man of his age flying.

"A bunch of friends of mine said they figured they'd have to take a day off soon and go to my funeral," remembers Charlie. "Well, I've attended all of theirs now."

Charlie, who has three great-grandchildren, bills himself to friends as "The Flying Great-Grandfather." A longtime member of the Minnesota Flying Farmers, he flies to air shows and to the Dakotas to hunt deer with his bow and arrow. And he makes regular trips to visit his children and grandchildren.

One day recently, he and his wife, Marjorie, flew to Brookings, S.D., to visit a daughter, and then flew home the same day.

Charlie, who has logged well over 3,000 hours in the air, never has had a mishap in an airplane. He's a careful pilot, keeps his plane well-maintained and never tries to stretch his fuel.

"You take Rapid City (S.D.), for instance. It takes about 46 gallons of fuel to get there from Mabel. My plane holds 50, so you'd figure I could make it. Not me. I refuel about halfway. I'm in no hurry anyway."

And take Minneapolis. "I wouldn't drive a car to Minneapolis for anything. But I don't mind flying in there."

Charlie reads all the aviation publications he can get. "I want to keep up on what's new in equipment and things. And it keeps my brain alive."

It's easier for him to fly these days.

He used to have to follow highways and rivers and other landmarks to get where he's going. Now, with all his radio equipment, he just locks onto a radio beam.

"Then she just kind of goes by herself."

How long can Charlie keep flying?

Well, there's an old saying among veteran pilots: You fly until the day comes you can't climb into a plane anymore.

I'd say that might happen to Charlie at 110. Maybe.

August 12, 1984

Ever tried to bash a rubber mouse?

I have a hunch that during all of July there was a full moon. And every day of that month was Friday the 13th.

For some reason, my July was weird. There are wags, of course, who will say that I'm the one who's weird. I retaliate by sticking pins in their little dolls.

Nothing horrendous happened to me. It was a series of minor things.

For one thing, I had close encounters with a dozen or more cars. The drivers were particularly aggressive and vicious, I thought.

I had all sorts of trouble with mechanical gadgets. One evening I dialed a phone number on the television remote control. And then put it to my ear.

We have a video cassette recorder and we also have cable TV. There was a particular movie I wanted to tape and watch at the same time. This means you can remove the commercials with a remote control gadget.

I carefully hooked up the thing, turned on the TV and poised myself to X out the first group of commercials. My wife, Janet, kept giving me stranger looks than usual.

We watched the movie for about 25 minutes, and I said:

"Boy, they're really giving us a break on commercials."

"Hey, Big Dummy," said Janet, "it's a cable channel that doesn't have commercials."

There was a terrible thunderstorm one morning and the electricity went out about 8 a.m. for 15 minutes. I fixed all the electric clocks, but forgot about the coffeemaker, which has a clock on it.

That evening, Janet asked me to set that straight. It was about 8 p.m. I set the coffeemaker clock ahead 15 minutes, then commented:

"What luck! It's a good thing it was 8, or I would have had to set it ahead hours."

Janet patiently told me that no matter when I set it, I only had to put it ahead 15 minutes. It took me quite a while to figure that out.

October 13, 1985

ROBERT T SMITH

Then there was a varmint in our back yard. Some burrowing animal made a hole at the edge of our driveway. I stuck a stick in the hole and we went away for the weekend.

When I returned, the stick was gone and there was this black, ugly, awful head and shoulders sticking out of the hole. I got a baseball bat and whacked the monster repeatedly.

Have you ever tried to bash a rubber mouse? (I learned later that our neighbor, Bill O'Donnell, did it. He stays young by playing tricks on me. He says he likes me a lot because I'm so gullible. There was the time, for instance, when he got my Sunday *Star and Tribune* early in the morning and switched pages around so, in my space, Sid Hartman's column appeared. Bill said he thought I would like more readership.)

Never have I had, or even witnessed, a hole-in-one. Well, in July I did. My friend, Bob Sorenson, who used to run the Little Wagon in Minneapolis, did it—and it was weird.

He hit a 5-wood on a 158-yard par 3 (we're not very strong anymore). The ball hit well before the green, rolled forever, then stopped at the edge of the cup. And it stayed stopped. It seemed like 15 seconds. Then, as if bored, it just fell in.

My son, Bryan, 8, got a little weird one night. We were driving home and he began to speak: "You know the government knows a lot about people. The FBI does, too."

Then he turned to Janet and proclaimed: "You know, Mom, they even know that you're short."

In the middle of a July night, our doorbell rang. It's one of those gimmicky deals that plays tunes. You can select anything from "The Beer Barrel Polka" to "When the Saints Go Marchin' In."

I answered the door and no one was there, but the doorbell was still playing "You've Got to Be a Football Hero" over and over.

Have you ever tried to disconnect a doorbell while half asleep?

Perhaps the topper was the July day I went to the funeral of Arnie Pearson, an old friend who used to work for the Associ-

ated Press. I was told it was at Lakewood Cemetery.

I arrived at Lakewood chapel on time and started down the aisle. People looked at me rather strangely, and then an usher approached me.

"Are you a friend of Mrs. Kinske?" he whispered.

You see, Arnie's funeral was at graveside.

October 13, 1985

Ethel is not run of the mill

Ethel Furne, 76, who ran for 6 hours and 6 minutes in the Twin Cities Marathon, finishing first in a class by herself.

OK, so some dude from Iowa won the Twin Cities Marathon. He got the money and the glory and the big write-ups.

And what did Ethel Furne get? A lousy T-shirt.

The Iowa guy did the 26.2 miles in a bit over two hours and 10 minutes. But he's a kid, only 31.

Ethel, who is 76, ran for 6 hours and 6 minutes plus—more than four hours longer than the Iowa finish.

The Iowa guy has been running for many years. Ethel didn't start running until she was 74, for crying out loud.

She finished next to last in the official listing. But she was first in her class, as determined by age group and gender.

OK, she was the only one in that class.

Ethel, one of 18 kids in her family, was born on a farm near Wabasha, Minn. She and her husband Lowell, 72, still live in that riverside town.

She was husking corn and pitching hay probably before the Iowa guy's parents were born.

"There weren't enough girls in our family and I was a tomboy, so I worked as a farmhand," Ethel told me in her Wabasha home. "Was as good as any male around. I've been an outdoor girl all my life."

The Iowa flash works at the ADM plant in Clinton. Inside.

After marrying, Ethel continued her outdoor activities. She biked regularly to

79

Lake City, Winona and Durand, Wis. Then she took up water skiing. In her 50s, she decided downhill skiing would be fun.

Two years ago the Wabasha County Fair offered a one-mile race for senior citizens. Ethel decided to try it. She won going away.

And for that, Twin Cities Marathon chiefs, she got a trophy.

Ethel took to running like a horse takes to sugar, and she was running 5 miles every other day when it was suggested that she enter the marathon.

The longest she ever had run was 18 miles, on her 75th birthday, and she did it in nine-minute miles. That's pretty fair speed, as any jogger will verify.

To warm up for the marathon, Ethel again did 18 miles two weeks before the race.

Then came the big day. "I started out and felt good," she said. "Then some nephews and nieces joined me from time to time on the route. That cheered me up. I was determined to finish."

Ethel doesn't go all out for the 26.2 miles. She runs, then slows down to what she says is "a bit faster than a slow jog." Then she runs again. She estimates she ran about 20 of the 26.2 miles.

She never stopped. Well, once—to go to the bathroom.

"When I finished there were 30 of my friends and relatives to greet me," said Ethel. "They gave me a red rose. That was a big lift."

She was a bit sore after the big race, but some liniment and rubbing did the trick. Next day she was out running again.

Aside from running, Ethel has her morning workout: 400 rounds on an exercycle, 200 jumps on her trampoline, 20 situps, and then waistbends.

Bet that Iowa guy won't be doing that at 76.

Ethel is 5 feet 5, weighs a trim 130 pounds. Now, I guess you have to give the Iowa flash credit for his win. I mean, I did a middle-aged shuffle for a 10K race about a year ago, and I still feel it.

But Ethel's a little disappointed. "A T-shirt, that's all I got," she told me. "I'm waiting for a big check." She was kidding about that.

In all, Twin Cities Marathon chiefs, Ethel has got nine trophies and 17 medals for her running.

And a T-shirt.

January 12, 1986

Jeffrey: he knew he was special

Jeffrey Anhalt Jr. was never supposed to crawl, certainly not to walk. He was thought to be brain-damaged and doctors gave him little chance of ever talking.

Well, he did it all. And he did it with smiles and courage and stubbornness.

Jeffrey died shortly before Christmas after only 2½ years of life. But his mother, Kathy, 36, wants people to know about his life.

One reason is that she believes that, without the help of *Minneapolis Star and Tribune* readers, and others, Jeffrey's life might have been much shorter.

Jeffrey was born with a lot of problems. His heart was a disaster—only one ventricle, a severely-narrowed aorta, no mitral valve, a hole between the two top heart chambers and a pulmonary artery four times too large.

It was an extremely rare case. He might not have lived more than six hours after his birth.

The family situation was complicated by state, federal and county red tape. Kathy, a registered nurse, and her husband, Jeffrey Sr., a machinist from Chaska, worked hard but did not have enough income for their son's medical costs.

But they weren't poor enough for welfare. Such people are called "the gray poor."

Their plight was aired in this column and people came to their aid, financially and emotionally. The state and Hennepin County also gave in and provided a Family Subsidy Grant.

It allowed Jeffrey Jr. to get proper medical care including expensive operations.

January 12, 1986

ROBERT T SMITH

But, most important of all, it allowed the boy to be at home with his parents.

Although still not at all out of danger, Jeffrey Jr. grew to be 3 feet tall and to weigh 30 pounds. He was always behind schedule in terms of normal childhood development, but he crawled when he was about a year old and walked at 2.

His mind proved to be perfectly all right.

Kathy and Jeffrey Sr. packed a lot into the 2½ years. Young Jeffrey went fishing often with his father, visited zoos, the Minnesota State Fair, the North Shore of Lake Superior, among other things.

"He seemed to know he was special," said his mother. "He never expected anyone to respond to him in a negative way and no one did. He was so happy."

And, she said, he taught her a lot.

"He taught me never to give up. Every gain he made was after many, many hours of struggle for him. But he never quit. He did all the things people thought he never would do.

"He taught me courage. He went through a lot of pain, vomited a lot, but he was no complainer. He had a wisdom far beyond his age.

"All my life I never thought I did anything quite right. But concerning him, with his help, I feel I did it right. He taught me that.

"He taught me to appreciate each day. He enjoyed all the little things of life. He savored each day, and he had such a sunny personality. He just seemed to accept all his problems and go right on."

Kathy wants to thank "all the people who reached out to a child they didn't know."

People sent money to the Anhalts, but they did more. A Minneapolis couple went to the Anhalt house occasionally and cooked meals. A nurse offered to care for the boy when the Anhalts needed to get out for an evening. Sen. Rudy Boschwitz got after federal government agencies.

There were many more.

"No matter what anyone says, there still are people in this world who care, people who gave a little boy something

of themselves, people who reached out to strangers," Kathy Anhalt said.

Ironically, Jeffrey died during minor surgery at Minneapolis Children's Medical Center. He had been running a high temperature for some time and doctors wanted to run a test on him.

They gave him a bit of anesthetic, the same used during other more serious operations. This time he couldn't handle it.

"They put him in my arms and no one in that operating room left until I put him down," said his mother.

Jeffrey's grandfather, Paul Turner, spoke at the boy's funeral.

"From the first days of your difficult life," he said, "you brightened the lives of all who were fortunate to know you. Somehow you had a special grasp of the world about you, a grasp seldom seen in a small child . . ."

Get rid of one bag of complications a day

Not long ago, Jon Hassler, author of such fascinating novels as *Staggerford*, arrived at a party in south Minneapolis. It was populated mainly by reporters, authors, editors and college professors.

Hassler mingled a bit, then seemed to be looking for someone. He noticed Majel White and approached her. They talked for more than a half hour.

He had never met her before.

I wasn't surprised they talked that long. Majel, who kept protesting that she didn't belong with "such swells," is an earth mother in an age of electronic gadgets and too many cardboard people.

She is shy and overly modest, but she has warmth and, at 59, an air of attractive girlish naivete. Hassler, I'm sure, felt that.

Majel, a friend for years, is a nature lover, a romantic, a woman wise in a basic way. She sometimes lives in a fantasy world, but is more in touch with reality than most of us.

Whenever there's trouble, she is there. Not to baby you, but to help.

And she can make me laugh. Oh, she doesn't tell jokes. Just says things in her own unique way.

She always has white towels in her home "because it makes me feel I'm on vacation."

She loves candlelight "because it makes me feel 20 years younger and you don't have to dust."

She was on a train trip when a young woman. A guy tried to pick her up and it made her nervous. Her maiden name is Sommers, so when he asked her name she said: "Majel Winters."

She has six children and adores them all. But early in the marriage there wasn't a lot of money and she tells of how, after two kids, she gave her husband hot chocolate at night so he'd fall asleep. It didn't work.

She also claims that, at night, she would pray, in terms of more children: "God in heaven, help me." After the fourth child, it became: "If there's a God in heaven, help me."

Majel, mostly a Minneapolis resident but now living in Grand Marais on the shore of Lake Superior, is well aware of waves and winds and wonders. Recently, she wrote to us:

"Yesterday, we saw a memorable sight. The lake had a thin layer of ice floating on top, with the wind doing a number on it.

"Squares of ice about a half-inch thick were washing to shore and, when the pile got to a certain height, the squares slid down on newly formed ice.

"The sun was shining and the ice was aquamarine, and the sound was like shimmering chandeliers."

Born in Eden, S.D., Majel was the daughter of the mayor of the town (population 132). The Depression drove the family to Minneapolis, where Majel met and married Bob White, a postal employee who now is a professional photographer.

After 30 years of wedlock, Bob still keeps trying to get Majel all to himself. But with her interest in family and people in general, it's not easy.

Majel sometimes appears a bit absent-minded. There was the episode with the havarti cheese. Majel fell in love with it, saying, "It is as smooth as butter."

March 2, 1986

She invited some friends over one day and gave them crackers with "some wonderful cheese."

"Isn't it just as smooth as butter?" she asked.

"But, Majel, it *is* butter," they replied.

Once when she was in the bathtub, a Bible salesman came to the door. One of her kids informed her of the visit. Always polite, Majel rushed to the door to greet the salesman. In the nude.

One of her favorite words is serious, as in, "That's a serious hammer you have there."

Her romanticism strays from trains to white linen tablecloths with a vase containing a single rose.

She is a strong believer in simplifying her life. As she tells her children: "Get rid of one bag of complications a day."

The nature woman learned to drive in Lakewood Cemetery, and it is a special place for her. She taught my daughter, Amy, to drive there.

Without notice, she will pack a picnic lunch and grab her husband and spend an afternoon among the dead.

She has always maintained, and proved, that the most special times are when you are with people one-on-one.

Jon Hassler found that out.

March 2, 1986

Holly: a very special trouper

You enter the Itasca Recreation Association Arena and start looking for Holly. Normally, burly high-school hockey players are slamming each other against the boards, but not this day.

You see a sign: "The 13th Annual Minnesota Special Olympics Winter Games." It's mainly a skiing and skating competition for the mentally retarded, some of whom have other problems.

You find Holly Colwell, 16, who for seven years has been preparing for this day. She started at the figure-skating school at Braemar Arena in Edina, and more recently has taken private lessons.

Twice a week for those seven years Holly, who was born with Down's syndrome, has practiced her skating.

You remember writing about Holly when she was 5. She had graduated from Project EDGE, an experimental program at the University of Minnesota. And you have followed her since.

Her parents, Dave and Char Colwell, of Edina, were told in the beginning to expect practically nothing of Holly. They didn't believe it.

You remember that she went to Countryside Elementary School as the first Down's syndrome child in the Edina school system. She was in a special resource room and learned to read at age 8.

You remember Dave saying, "There was a time they were telling us this would never happen. Well, hell, there was a time when they said she'd never be toilet trained, and she's sitting there reading to me out of a first-grade book."

She reads at the fifth-grade level now.

You think of more progress she's made—all of it costing a great deal of hard work. She's now in Valley View Junior High and is mainstreamed in art, music, physical education, home economics and typing. She can type 40 words a minute.

You read the winter games program a bit: "Our athletes have trained long hours in preparation for the games. . . . They are now ready for the ultimate challenge in sports competition. Today, these individuals finally come together to experience what they've all been waiting for—a chance to put forth their best effort, to test their skills, to learning something new . . ."

You watch the figure-skating contestants warming up. No, they'll never make the Ice Follies, but you remember how far they had to come just to be able to do what they're doing.

You chat with Randy Westerham, state Special Olympics program director: "It's a growing thing for them. And most important is the carry-over. They achieve something like this in sports, something they enjoy. It builds up their confidence, and then they start learning other things. It's not just to win a medal."

The competition begins. Each girl must pass the compulsory movements. You watch Hope, 11, of St. Louis Park, and she falls down. She gets up and starts over. This time she does it.

Then the big event. Each girl does a free-style show, with her own music. For Holly's group, the routine must include seven movements, including a backward swizzle and a snowplow stop. It can include anything else.

You watch Hope. She begins her routine, then stops. She can't remember the rest. She begins to weep and leaves the ice. You figure she tried, and that was great.

But about 10 minutes later, Hope is back. She's going to try again.

You cross your fingers and, with the others, cheer her on. This time she does it all. The applause is gigantic. You give Hope the medal for courage.

Then it's Holly's turn. You watch her stand perfectly straight in her bright pink costume with the sparkling sequins on it. She extends her arms.

Her music is Herb Alpert's "Tijuana Taxi." You see Holly begin, a bit tentatively, and then she twirls four times. She's now getting into it.

You see this girl, who wasn't supposed to even get toilet trained, do a hop step, a windmill motion, a one-legged swoop, other movements.

You are proud of this girl, whose parents just wouldn't believe she couldn't succeed at anything.

The awards ceremony copies the grown-up Olympics. All the athletes win a medal. You listen as the winners are named— fourth runner-up, third runner-up.

Holy is named second-best in the state in her division.

You notice that she's disappointed, and you figure that it is good that she's competitive. The disappointment does not last long.

You leave the arena thinking about these young people, and about others who are "normal" and who take that for granted. Others who squander their talents because they won't work hard.

You say to Holly, not out loud: "Hey, great going, kid. You showed those experts who said you'd never make much out of life. You showed 'em."

March 6, 1986

I shouldn't have put out the fire

It has four wheels and is bigger than a breadbox and it has taught me how to hate. It's Clarence, my 1976 Pontiac Sunbird.

I bought Clarence second-hand four years ago. I knew nothing of his parentage or upbringing. Now, I suspect that the original owner of Clarence delighted in mistreating him.

But why does he have to take it out on me?

There are some little things wrong with Clarence. They're annoying, but you can live with them. Take the fact that no matter what you buy or do, the windshield wipers merely smear the rain about a bit.

In the winter, Clarence is diabolical. Each day he decides whether or not he will start. If he didn't start at all, one could do something. Maybe buy a new battery.

But Clarence will start maybe two or three days in the row and then decide to take a day off. And you never know when he'll do that.

I take that back. I should know, because it is always on a day when I need him the most.

The worst problem with Clarence is he's as lazy as a hound dog in the sun. He has all the get-up-and-go of a glued slug.

He dawdles from zero to 20 miles an hour and then takes his sweet time to get up to 40. Then you have no idea what he will do.

Sometimes, he will get right with it and hit the 55 mile an hour speed limit in prime time. Other times, he will stay at 40. Other times than that, he will slow down. It doesn't matter what you are doing with the gas pedal.

As you can imagine, I am as popular with freeway motorists as a nearsighted dentist with the palsy.

I took Clarence one day to one of those high-tech places where they attach computers to everything and then tell you what's wrong. Well, they presented me with a bill for $87 and said: "Your car is tired."

"He gets enough sleep," I said.

"Sorry, there's nothing to be done," they said. I'm convinced Clarence somehow faked the tests.

Clarence doesn't like me to play golf, which I love. I try to do it on Saturday mornings. Clarence figures out ways to stop me.

A while back, Clarence was dripping all over the streets. Seems he needed a new water pump. Cost: $126.

The following Saturday morning, as I was tootling off to golf, Clarence stopped on the Crosstown. Never said a word, just stopped.

Tow charge: $30. Clarence had somehow struggled out of his fanbelt, then chewed it up. Cost: $85.

Just a week or so ago, I was again on the way to golf. This time Clarence put on his Add Coolant sign. So, I stopped at a station and added some.

A few miles later, just to be ornery, he turned the sign on again. At the second station, a mechanic examined Clarence and, with what seemed like glee, announced: "The head gasket is busted." Cost: $193.

I've tried talking nice to Clarence, but it does no good. I've tried snubbing him by taking a bus. It just makes him meaner.

My last resort is to tell him about LeRoy. If Clarence doesn't shape up, I'm going to do it.

LeRoy was another car I had. I murdered him. He had many of the same maddening characters as Clarence. LeRoy's best trick was to get stuck in a quarter-inch of snow.

In January of 1979, he did it on the edge of downtown Minneapolis. I went a bit mad. I kept running the engine and LeRoy kept spinning his wheels. Finally, the engine got too hot and steam spewed from the hood. I left LeRoy there and, looking back, noticed flames.

"Already hell," I thought.

There's a feeling of power after a murder, you know. I was hoping no one heard me screaming "fiend" at LeRoy during the slaying.

Regaining a bit of cool, I decided it would be dangerous perhaps to let that fire go. So, I returned and, with some snow, put it out.

LeRoy was towed to my service station and a mechanic looked him over. All the mechanic said was:

"You shouldn't have put out that fire."

April 5, 1986

Charlie gets all clear to die

When I arrived at the tiny apartment near 15th and Park, Charlie was carefully putting things into a bushel basket.

I had known Charlie for a long time. He was a retired baker, an 86-year-old man with no living relatives. He had never married and thus had no children. His life, a quiet, gentle one, was centered on friends in his neighborhood, many of them elderly. The short, pudgy man, with just meager arches of white hair winding over his ears, was shy.

"Now, remember," he said as I entered the apartment, "no names if you write about anything. I'm not looking for publicity."

Charlie already had told me what it was about: He was going to die. A bad heart and leukemia and old age.

He didn't want anybody to know. "Don't want any pity and people fussing about me," he said. But Charlie wanted his friends to have the possessions he valued. "Otherwise someone will just probably throw them away," he said. The monetary value of what he was packing in the bushel basket was very small. No jewelry, no silverware, no first editions.

Charlie finished his packing and stood up. "It's time to go now," he said. He had called me to help carry the basket.

Outside it was evening and cool. Charlie held one handle of the basket and I the other. We first went to a nearby home for the elderly. A woman with bluish-gray hair answered the door of one apartment.

"Well, Charlie," she said, "how nice. Come in."

"I can't stay, Annie," said Charlie. "I've just been kinda cleaning out my place and I found something I'd like to give you."

He pulled an old Bible out of the basket.

ROBERT T SMITH

September 7, 1986

He handed it to Annie. "It belonged to my grandmother and then my mother," he said. "I'm too old to need a Bible anymore. But you're still young enough."

Annie, who must be in her 70s, laughed. "Are you sure you don't want it?" she asked.

"Yeah, I'm sure," he said.

The next stop, in the same building, was to the apartment of an elderly man. For him, Charlie pulled out a scarf with his initials embroidered on it.

"You're always complaining about your neck being cold, Henry, and I found this old scarf in a drawer," said Charlie. "So quit your bitching now." Henry invited us in for coffee, but Charlie said he'd come back some other time. "I've got some other junk I've got to get rid of," he said.

Then a small, run-down house where a divorced woman lives with her 8-year-old son, Jerry. The boy visited Charlie regularly and ran errands for him.

Jerry answered the door. "Hi," he said, "if you needed something why didn't you call?" Charlie gave him his getting-rid-of-junk explanation and gave Jerry an old pocket watch. Jerry had admired the watch previously and it was obvious he was excited to have it.

"But you need it," the boy said.

Charlie laughed and said: "Who needs to know the time at my age."

And so it went. Thirteen items in all. The last went to a young woman who lives with her husband in the same apartment building as Charlie did. The old man handed her a picture—of himself.

"The frame is good," said Charlie. "You can use it for any picture you want."

The woman looked at Charlie for what seemed like a long time. "What's going on, Charlie?" she asked, gently. "I don't buy the junk bit."

"Tell your husband it's a picture of your secret love," said Charlie and they both laughed.

As we left, the woman said: "The frame won't be used for another picture, Charlie."

Three weeks later, Charlie died in his sleep.

September 7, 1986

Legal racing
hurts illegal bookies

Bennie the Bookie, who trolls 4th St., is upset these days. Seems that the annual fall sport of illegal betting on football has hit sort of a recession.

And the villain is, according to Bennie, Canterbury Downs.

"I'm down 20 percent and Lenny the Loon is down 25," said Bennie. "Other guys are crying the same blues."

Before the thoroughbred racetrack opened, sports gambling in the Twin Cities area amounted to $100 million a year, according to the FBI estimate. Most of that was on football.

We were seventh in the nation in illegal sports wagering.

Ben Patty, FBI special agent and spokesman, said: "I wouldn't be surprised if football gambling was down" because of Canterbury, but he said there are no new figures as yet.

So, at least for the moment, the $100 million estimate stands.

He did not argue with Bennie's theory that there is only so much gambling money available in an area and the take at Canterbury could come out of the pockets of football bookies.

There are always those addicted who would bet the sun won't rise tomorrow. But they are not a major part of the gambling public, just as alcoholics are not a major part of the drinking public.

"But the ordinary people who gamble have sort of a budget for that," said Bennie. "There's only so much money they'll risk in a year. And the ordinary people are the bulk of our business."

(Another bookie agreed with Bennie, but said there might be another reason for the slump. "There isn't the huge interest in pro football that there used to be," he said. "The television audience is down, and more and more people are doing something else on Sunday afternoons. In the good old days, you couldn't blast a guy away from watching the pros.")

I asked Bennie why the bookies didn't

go into illegal off-track betting. It exists around most major racetrack areas.

"There was a little flurry at first," said Bennie. "But it wasn't organized and there were too many problems with the customers."

No bookie, for instance, would pay more than 15 to 1 on a horse. If you bet $100 on a 100-to-1 shot at the track, and he won, you'd get $10,000. From the bookie, you'd get only $1,500.

And bookies won't handle daily double or exacta type bets, the ones that can pay off big.

"Customers had a lot of trouble with that stuff," said Bennie.

Phil Jones, of the Minneapolis police vice squad, said there is no indication that off-track betting to any extent is going on in this area.

"We've had not one complaint since the track opened," said Jones.

FBI Agent Patty said he could not comment on any ongoing investigation, but "no federal charge has been made in Minnesota" against anyone engaged in off-track betting.

Neither Jones nor Patty could say there is no such thing. But whatever might be going on is probably very minor.

I suggested to Bennie that things might pick up after the track closes this fall.

"Maybe," he said, "but the customers we've lost to the track are not going to bet more on football than they normally do.

"It's like you're running a gas station and a customer goes on vacation for three months. He doesn't come back and double his gas order. You've just lost three months of his business."

Maybe, I told Bennie, he should get into another business. Something legal.

He looked at me as though I had suggested he set his hair on fire. Then he shrugged and continued down 4th St.

August 2, 1987

High Rise Joe: a blind man who sees a lot

It's the last listing of the white pages in the Minneapolis telephone book: Zzzzyzzer-rific Funline, 1355 Nicollet Av. . . . 870-1111. It's for kids and it belongs to High Rise Joe.

High Rise Joe Engressia, 38, lives at that address and the kids who dial that number get about 15 minutes of everything from nonsense to a serious story about the Holocaust.

It's also listed in the phone book under Dial-a-Funline. It's not like other dial-a's which cost 50 cents for a few seconds. This one is on High Rise Joe.

"How can you charge kids for anything?" he says.

High Rise is totally blind, from birth, and lives alone. He claims it is fun to be crazy "because if not I'd miss so many things." So would the kids.

An example of what you might hear on Funline:

"Today boys and girls I have for sale a T-shirt on which is emblazoned: Valleyfair is A Pi'u. A pi'u is Italian for a plus. They are invisible and cost only 10,000 invisible dollars.

"You can buy one with invisible money and a main advantage is they don't clutter up your closet."

High Rise says that, if your friends can't see the shirt, it's their loss. He told me that you can't make such an offer to adults. They wouldn't understand.

But kids? "One called me and asked if he could put the cost of the shirt on his invisible Master Card."

The "money" from the sale of the T-shirts, incidentally, goes to a High Rise creation: "Silent Films for the Blind."

High Rise, who was born in Richmond, Va., had a radio talk show in Denver until the station made it an all-music show. He had such guests as the last person to own a crank telephone in the nation. He came to Minneapolis in 1982.

ROBERT T SMITH

September 13, 1987

He creates all sorts of things for his kids. Diet shampoo for fatheads. Candy-flavored shoes for one who puts his foot in his mouth. His slogan: "Help keep the world safe for nonsense."

His funline show is recorded. But if a kid wants, he can call High Rise Joe at 870-7070 for a personal talk. Among others, High Rise specializes in terminally ill kids.

There was Ronnie, who died at 13. High Rise talked with him on the phone regularly for the last six months of his life.

"He was my teacher," said High Rise. "Always so joyous and excited. He told me of graduating from eighth grade, of learning Russian. Well, not always so joyous and excited . . ."

Ronnie called one day and said he was tired of people trying to cheer him up and would High Rise say something sad. Without hesitation, High Rise began:

"Do you know what happens when people take the caps off of pens and forget to replace them? They suffocate. They die slowly. And what about dinner rolls that come in a connected bunch? You take two or three of them and rip them away from the pack. And eat them. The pack is then sad and lonely without their pals . . ." Ronnie loved it.

High Rise gets about 1,000 calls a week for his recorded show—which he changes every week. He gets around town with a cane called EDITH, which translates to "Early Detection of Idiotic Tripping Hazards."

He claims to be an eternal child and loves the way kids say things.

Not long ago, he was walking with EDITH in a skyway and a mother and child approached. The boy said: "Mother, that man's blind."

Said Mother: "Shhhssss."

Said Junior: "What's the matter, doesn't he know he's blind?"

High Rise thought that was right on.

The blind man lives on Social Security and has a hobby of helping phone companies. He says he's an expert, that he can dial a number and, through sound alone, tell if there's any trouble on the circuit.

He once dialed a New York City number and determined that all the long-distance phone calls were not being charged to the caller or anyone. He phoned that particular telephone office and told them. They didn't believe him.

So, he informed an executive and he checked. Yep, High Rise was right. That's only one story about his telephone prowess.

He knows all the jargon. He will call a phone office and say such things as: "On your A.I.S trunks, they're giving offhook supervision, causing one-minute bill errors. Need to change the S.T.I. on BCT trunk group to 24." That one saved the customers money.

But mostly High Rise deals with kids. There was Jason, in a coma for a long time. His mother asked High Rise to sing something to him. High Rise made up a song about peanut butter and the mother held the phone to Jason's ear.

Maybe it was just time for Jason to come to, but after the song he said his first words since the coma: "Peanut butter . . ."

I'll take a dozen of those $10,000 T-shirts.

September 13, 1987

Nicollet Hotel was a city palace

For all those who remember, and those too young to have known . . .

It was a Minneapolis palace, a place where young brides had their receptions, where couples celebrated their anniversaries and where millionaires noted their financial coups.

It was a place where a young senator, John Kennedy, held court for reporters in the Jolly Miller bar.

I inquired if he were going to run for president.

He said: "Ask my father." Everyone laughed.

It was a place nestled in the heart of the skid row district of Minneapolis and yet it remained the class of the city.

Now, they are trying to make the Nicollet Hotel an historical site. I hope they do. Thursday, the State Review Board for the National Register of Historic Places voted

October 4, 1987

to put the Nicollet on the register. It still has to be approved by the National Park Service and the state historic preservation officer, but the big hurdle has been leaped.

Aside from recordings, I was first introduced to the music of Glenn Miller, Artie Shaw, Tommy Dorsey, Gene Krupa and, oh yeah, Lawrence Welk, in the elegant Minnesota Terrace of the Nicollet.

One reason I play the trumpet today—albeit badly—is that Bunny Berrigan, the greatest, once played "I Can't Get Started" at the Nicollet.

The hotel made the career of a little known Milwaukee songstress, Hildegarde. People here loved her and packed the place whenever she came.

It was where I first saw my first love, Judy Garland, in person. I was 16. She was two years older.

It was where you could see women in long gowns with furs and jewels and men in tuxedos sporting $5 cigars.

It was where you could go to feel as if you weren't as unimportant as you were.

Several presidents stayed there, including Harry Truman and Dwight Eisenhower. Others who checked in more than once were actor James Stewart and Adlai Stevenson and Averill Harriman.

For less than $10, you could order squab and caviar and a fine Chateau Margaux bordeaux. If all you wanted was a filet mignon, you'd have to cough up $1.35. Plus tip, of course.

In fairness, that was in the 1930s and early 40s. Later, the filet would have cost you $3.50.

The Nicollet was the family hotel of the Roosevelts. They never stayed anywhere else while in Minneapolis. Once, reported Sam Bratman, who was catering manager, Eleanor Roosevelt was in town and it was her birthday.

Sam ordered up a huge cake for a reception for Eleanor. There were swinging doors to the kitchen and the waiter carrying the cake collided with a waiter coming the other way. Sam did what he had to: He held up the reception until another cake could be created.

Said Eleanor: "You'd never get such consideration in Washington."

The Minneapolis Aquatennial was born in the Nicollet. And most of the civic groups—the Kiwanis, the Rotary, Northwest Variety—met there regularly. They would meet no other place.

The hotel produced its own ice and mix, had its own laundry and bakery and butcher shop and you could order up a barber or beautician to your room within minutes.

Despite its class, the Nicollet never lost its warmth and knew it was a place in the Midwest, not on New York's Central Park West.

Maybe it was World War II that killed the Nicollet. I don't know. But it never was the same after the war. And the palace slowly declined. Finally, in 1973, the Nicollet died.

I conducted my own funeral. The English renaissance style hotel was a derelict. I wandered through the place, now run down. I looked into what had been the Minnesota Terrace, no longer a first rate night club. Just an empty, dusty room.

I heard, or thought I did, Glenn Miller's theme song. And I saw, or thought I did, a beautiful woman in a long white gown.

I knew that a part of this city's history was gone. I knew there never would be another Nicollet.

October 4, 1987

A marriage envied in heaven

Finally it became clear to these 17- going on 18-year-old people that fate had intended them for each other—and with the certainty that this age group has—they decided that they were meant for each other and became engaged to be married—even though they had never met.

from "A Remarkable Woman"

It was World War I and those two young lovers are now Jasper and May Hammond. They have been for almost 68 years.

A headline in the *Star Tribune* on Friday read: "84% of women in study unhappy with relationships." Jasper, 86, and

ROBERT T SMITH

October 4, 1987

May, 87, know nothing about such problems.

And Jasper wants folks to know about their marriage. So he wrote a booklet called "A Remarkable Woman." It's not for sale. He just gives it away.

"I want everybody to know what a gal she really is," says the former chairman of the board of Franklin Manufacturing Co. of St. Cloud, Minn. "It's my tribute to her."

It's also a delightful love story about a woman who lost no spirit during bad financial times, who is at home in the wilderness or in a Washington, D.C. drawing room, and who isn't called One Shot May for nothing.

She has felled Kodiak bears with one shot, once when that's all the time she had. And as Jasper writes in his booklet (He calls her Our Lady.):

"Our Lady (at 60) wanted to bag a caribou and her husband was very proud as he watched her, and the guide, crawling on their bellies over the arctic tundra on the arctic shore, cradling the rifle expertly in her arms. When the caribou jumped and ran after the shot she was afraid she had missed. But it ran about 200 yards and dropped dead—a perfect heart shot."

The Hammond home in Little Canada is filled with trophies of the hunting trips Jasper and May have made throughout the world.

They met when Jasper was in the U.S. Navy during World War I and May was in Chicago. Through a friend, they began to correspond by mail.

As Jasper writes: "Talk about wartime engagements not being permanent—all that was for others but not for this remarkable lady and her far-away sailor. If wartime romances never last then how about the chances of these two, who had never met each other and were separated by 2,000 miles of land and 3,000 miles of water?"

The Depression hit them hard, and Jasper, then a salesman, was worried about making enough money so they could eat. But May, then the mother of a girl, Elaine, kept Jasper's "drive and enthusiasm in top form."

In 1938, Jasper came to St. Paul to take a better job and his career took off. He finally became the chief executive of Franklin, then a huge, international freezer-manufacturing firm.

May had no trouble moving from a life of poverty to one of affluence. Jasper went to Washington during World War II to become a special consultant to the War Production Board. It was one of those dollar-a-year jobs. May became a popular hostess.

Sometimes when they (politicians and big businessmen) were all together at dinner in glamorous wartime Washington, arguments would grow heated and almost dangerous. Then Our Lady would break in with a story about pheasant hunting in South Dakota or about the size and quantity of the lake trout, the northerns and the muskies found in Ontario. This would put the war effort back to maximum with the proper cooperation between government and industry.

Jasper, since retiring, has been the inspiration of a project in Arden Hills to get senior citizens to pay more attention to their health. It has been most successful at Johanna Shores, a long-term care center operated by Presbyterian Homes Foundation. The wellness program, emphasizing exercise and proper diet, started with the residents and then spread to the 400 employees. Jasper now is working to get the project on a national scale.

But the major part of his life still is May, who suffered a minor stroke recently. They will celebrate their 68th wedding anniversary on Christmas Eve. Jasper recalls when, in their 60s, they were marooned in the Arctic while on a canoe trip.

May handled it with all the courage of a young pioneer woman.

After all, she had her rifle.

Yeah, truly a remarkable woman.

April 10, 1988   ROBERT T SMITH

A baby grandson who got help

My newest grandson, Alexander Bangs, was born the morning of Feb. 20—two months early. He weighed but 4 pounds, and his heart and lungs were not fully developed.

He is the first child of my only daughter, Amy, and her husband, Chris Bangs, of south Minneapolis.

The situation with Alexander introduced

me to a project of sharing in the security of the life of a premature baby. It's the Infant Apnea Program of Minneapolis Children's Medical Center.

The night after Alexander was born, I visited him in a special ward of Children's. The first baby I saw was about the size of my hand. Yes, babies that small have survived. Alexander looked big in comparison.

My grandson is constantly on a monitor that records his breathing and heartbeats. If either stop, an alarm you can hear a block away goes off. He'll be on the monitor at least six months.

The Children's program was established to help the parents who, without that help, would be under the terrible strain of having to be "on duty" with their baby 24 hours a day.

It involves training people like me, who are designated by the parents to take care of babies like Alexander. I did the training with a friend, Lorna Sorensen. It's best to have two people on duty with the baby.

First, there are two hours of infant cardiopulmonary resuscitation (CPR), which is different for babies, particularly premature ones. Their bodies are so small that you must be very careful lest you break ribs or otherwise injure the child.

Each trainee is given a doll that responds to mouth-to-mouth resuscitation. They fill with air when receiving a breath. After instruction, we practiced infant CPR over and over again.

The trick is not so much learning how to perform the various techniques, but when to perform what. It makes a difference whether the baby is not breathing or the heart has stopped or both.

You also learn what to do if a baby is choking—while either conscious or unconscious.

There is an intensity in the instruction room. Everyone there represents the baby of a relative or friend. No one goofs off.

There follows about five hours of monitor training. Much of the time when the alarm sounds, the baby corrects the problem itself. But, if the baby's color has changed and the problem is not self-corrected, you have to go into action. Sometimes all it takes is a gentle nudge. The last resort is infant CPR. Then 911 is called.

The program, only two years old, costs the parents an initial fee. But the trainees pay nothing, and there is no limit to how many the parents can recruit.

"Our biggest need is awareness of the program," said Bonnie Brueshoff, coordinator of the project. "A lot of babies go home from hospitals on monitors with minimal instruction. Quality care is needed."

Lorna and I first baby-sat with Alexander on a Saturday. Amy and Chris were to make their first getaway since Alexander came home.

Alexander was now at 6 pounds. We watched the monitor, lights blinking for heartbeats and breaths. The alarm sounded several times during our stint, but Alexander corrected himself every time. He's tough.

Once, the alarm went off because one of the wires was disconnected. We fixed that.

I don't know how well we would have done if, say, infant CPR would have been necessary. But I know that even with routine alarms, it would have been terrifying without the training.

Alexander is doing fine, and there are now a dozen or so people trained to take care of him.

So, how did Amy and Chris enjoy their first getaway? Shortly after they left, Amy who has had the primary duty with Alexander, fell asleep and didn't wake up until the next morning. But that's what it's all about.

September 4, 1988

J. F. Powers: betting on god to win

Father broke into their kitchen as into a room of assassins, and confronted the glowering hulk of iron that was their stove.*

He is lean and modest, drives a 1973 Chrysler and lives in a humble gray stucco house built by monks in the 1920s. You might mistake him for a druggist.

But he's J. F. Powers, novelist and short-story writer, who has been ranked with James Joyce and Flannery O'Connor. About his novel that won the National Book Award. *Morte D'Urban,* Anthony Burgess commented: "The writing is superbly deadpan and the dialogue pure perfection."

The soft-spoken 71-year-old author, who seeks the limelight in the same manner as a mole, is easily one of America's leading serious writers. His latest novel, *Wheat That Springeth Green,* will be out the end of August.

As usual, the main character is a priest, located in central Minnesota in modern times. And, as usual, it's a priest with problems.

The calliope was not playing now, but

yesterday it had roamed the streets, all red and gold and glittering like a hussy among the pious, black Fords parked on the Square . . .*

James Farl Powers uses J. F. because he thinks his full name is too ordinary and because he has a couple of heroes: T. S. Eliot and S. J. Perelman. Powers has been working on the new novel since 1954. It was due in 1976, but he is a perfectionist.

In his usual self-deprecating manner, he says: "I'm a slow worker and a lazy person."

The author's fascination with priests prompted a question: Have you ever thought of being a priest yourself?

His answer: "I though a lot of not being a priest."

He said he uses priests because it's a way, in literary terms, to get on top of our society. "They are not different from the mass of people. Through them, you can see how society works." Or doesn't.

And Chastity, what of that? Well, that was all over for him—a battle he had fought and won many years ago. A sin whose temptations had prevailed undiminished through the centuries, but withal for him, an old man, a dead issue, a young man's trial.*

Powers, who teaches one creative writing course a year at St. John's University, grew up in Jacksonville, Ill., a college town. His stories have appeared in the likes of *The New Yorker;* his latest work is a Literary Guild alternate selection.

From his intellect and wit, you get the impression of a kid who was a bookworm and graduated from some snooty Eastern university. Wrong.

He was an athlete in high school—football, basketball, baseball—and never graduated from any college.

"I grew up in the Depression and there was no money for college. I spent most of the Depression looking for jobs, and I never seemed to land one."

He slapped himself fiercely on the back, missing the wily mosquito, and whirled to find it. . . . Then he saw it—oh, the preternatural cunning of it!—poised in the beard of St. Joseph on the bookshelf.*

Powers' first story was published in

November 27, 1988

ROBERT T SMITH

1943 in *Accent*, a small literary magazine. His first book, a collection of his short stories called *The Prince of Darkness*, came out in 1947.

He was way ahead of his time, in terms of writing about the Roman Catholic church. One satirical short story in *The New Yorker* caused an uproar. Called "Death of a Favorite," it was about the exorcism of a cat.

"They beat him with a crucifix," remembers Powers.

And the writer was dealing with priests and women long before almost any other writer.

Often his characters are losers, in terms of their ambitions and hopes. Asked if he is a cynic, Powers was a bit taken aback.

"Me, a cynic? Not at all. I'm betting on God to win. A lot of people are betting on him to show. And most people aren't betting on him at all."

Is he betting on people? "People are like horses. They tend to poop out in the stretch, or break a leg."

I like to sit in Grant Park and listen to the cops calling to each other like nightingales. You know the Chicago whistle? Wheeeeeeeeweeuhhhhhhheeeeeuhhhh... It'd scare the hell out of you—rightly played—if you didn't see the lights and the people and the Wrigley Building.*

Although a devout Catholic in terms of faith, Powers is not pleased with the church organization. "Just like the television networks, the church is in the ratings game. Everyone is selling to somebody else. And we don't even resent it anymore. We get numb."

The author's wife, Betty, died of cancer in May. They had five children; four of them live in Ireland, where the family spent many years. He is a jazz fan and a Minnesota Twins booster.

Snowflakes tumbled in feathery confusion, wonderfully white against the night, smothering the whole dirty, roaring, guilty city in innocence and silence and beauty.*

*Selections from the writings of J. F. Powers.

November 27, 1988

He was paid for his favorite hobby

It says a lot about the man. His favorite photo, which he took, is of a small deaf mute boy named Pippie who had just received a free pumpkin for Halloween.

"There was a glorious expression on his face," said the photographer. "It made you feel good."

And this from a man who was named National Newspaper Photographer of the Year three times—a feat not equaled before him or since. This from a man who has spent almost 42 years in the business.

This from Earl Seubert, a lovable, brown bear of a man with hands to match, who has photographed the Vietnam War twice and covered everything from murders to presidents to eight national political conventions.

Now, at 61, Earl, a friend and colleague since we both started on the *Minneapolis Daily Times* in 1947, is retiring as chief of photography of the *Star Tribune*.

Earl has won so many awards that he cannot tell you the number. The photographer of the year honor, which he won in 1953, 1955 and 1958, was bestowed by the University of Missouri School of Journalism, *Encyclopaedia Britannica* and the National Press Photographers Association.

Actually, Earl's not that impressed with awards. He'd rather tell you stories about being a news photographer.

• There was a time I was covering Haile

93

ROBERT T SMITH

November 27, 1988

Selassie right here in southern Minnesota. He was having lunch and all of a sudden he stood up. We all stood up. I thought he was through eating. But he had to go to the men's room. First time I every stood up for someone going to a men's room.

• President Eisenhower was fishing in the Black Hills. It was hot, hot, hot. We couldn't get near him, but I was the only photographer with a long lens. I got some pictures and developed them in a shack. I used an orange crate for a counter and had a blanket over me to shut out the light. It was about 150 degrees in the shade. Some of the negatives melted.

• We used to shoot all convicted drunk drivers in Minneapolis. We always got into fights. One day one of them came up to me before his trial, and said, 'You missed me the last time and you're gonna miss me again.' I said: 'Why not shoot you now?' He said 'You wouldn't do that!' BANG! I did.

Earl is a Minneapolis native. He played tackle on the South High School football team, then enlisted in the Navy in 1945. A year later, he studied business at the University of Minnesota. But he fell in love with Elaine, and needed more money than the G.I. Bill afforded. So he went in search of a job.

He has been taking pictures since he won a Baby Brownie camera in 1939 for selling subscriptions to the *Minneapolis Star-Journal*. He remembers one incident about being a carrier boy: "It was the horrible 1940 Armistice Day storm. I was late delivering the papers and one guy chewed me out royally."

Earl applied for a job at the Times on the day a photographer got fired. "I learned a lot about the news business in a hurry". He and Elaine were married and still are.

Because you can identify them with their cameras and other equipment, photographers sometimes are victims of attack. "I've been in just about every kind of riot there is. I've been poked by a bayonet, hit by rocks, police batons and once a cop threw a tear gas canister at me. In Chicago, I was hit by a bag of blue water. Didn't stain, didn't smell. Never did learn what it was."

What about fear? "It's strange, but with a camera in my hand, I'm not afraid." One night in Vietnam, Earl hid in a woods with small-arms fire all around him. "I was more scared of getting leeches in my pants."

The list of notables he has photographed is gigantic. Among them: presidents Eisenhower, Kennedy, Johnson, Nixon; celebrities Bing Crosby, Bob Hope, Natalie Wood, Arthur Godfrey, Eddie Cantor. Eddie Cantor? The shah of Iran, Prince Bertil of Sweden. Besides Vietnam, he has traveled Europe, Asia and Africa.

His colleagues have their own stories:

Photographer John Croft: "While he is a genius behind a camera, he might be even better in the darkroom. Lucky, too. Only Earl could put film in a developer timed for six to seven minutes and then take off for a half-hour coffee break. Then come back and have a most beautiful negative. Anybody else would have to shoot the assignment over."

Charlie Hoag of our advertising department: "I once gave Earl a hot tip on a picture during a major storm. Said Earl: 'Hoag, of all the hot tips you've given me, this is the stupidest.' The picture, however, was on a cover page the next morning."

Art Hager, retired *Star Tribune* photographer: "Earl always has been very professional and goes about his work with a great eye. He also enjoys a practical joke, especially if it is on someone else. Once I had to leave the office, and asked him to take my film out of the developer at the proper time. He pulled it on time, but hid it and substituted four sheets of fogged film."

So what makes a good newspaper photographer, besides knowing how to operate a camera? "You've got to enjoy people and events," Earl said. "You need some imagination, an eye for composition, to anticipate and to see things. Actually, I have been paid more than 40 years for practicing my favorite hobby."

As a reporter, I remember him often saying to me: "Well, Smith, I guess I've got to save your story again."

And so often he did.

June 11, 1989   ROBERT T SMITH

Halsey: set Scott's pants on fire

The memory of Halsey Hall has got to stay alive.

No one has taken his place as a storyteller. Some of his stories even were true.

Maybe not the one about the longest home run. Halsey would tuck the ever-present cigar in his mouth and say:

"It happened in Lake Norden, S.D. A first baseman hit the ball, and it landed in a gondola car of a passing train. Went all the way to Watertown, 25 miles away."

Or one he told sportscaster Ray Scott:

"I never like to say anything bad about anybody. Reminds me of the time a man who was generally disliked departed this world. At his funeral, no one could think of anything good to say about him—until his barber stepped forward and said: 'He was easy to shave.' See there's good in everyone."

To keep the Halsey memory alive, Hall fans will gather Monday, June 12, at Ray Scott's Sports Bar and Restaurant in Minneapolis. Scott will devote his hour-long radio sports talk show—5:30 to 6:30 p.m. on WWTC—to Halsey.

Scott is a big fan of Halsey, despite the fact that the legend of sportswriting and broadcasting once set Scott on fire.

It happened during a Minnesota Twins game radio broadcast. Scott and Halsey were in the broadcast booth, and Halsey, in the process of lighting a cigar, dropped a lighted match, igniting some ticker tape and Scott.

"Ever try to do play-by-play with your pants on fire?" said Scott.

On hand at the restaurant to tell Halsey stories will be Calvin Griffith, former long-time owner of the Twins, who, after Halsey died 11 years ago, said: "Hell, yes, I miss him. There never was a time when things were going bad for me that a cheery note didn't arrive from Halsey."

Also invited are a bunch of Halsey buddies of newspapering. Bill Hengen, Dick Gordon, Jimmy Byrne, Tom Briere and Bob Beebe. Others will include Tom Mee, George Brophy, Arno Goethel and Herb Carneal. Any other Halsey fans or friends will be welcome.

It was impossible not to like old Halsey, who put in 57 years in the sports reporting business and died at age 79. He was totally unassuming; he once wore two different-colored shoes to a fancy party. He forgot his belt on one baseball trip and used a length of rope. As he was getting out of a car in front of the fashionable Beach Hotel in Melbourne, Fla., the rope broke. Halsey caught the pants at half-mast.

I was a young reporter on the *Minneapolis Tribune,* working nights for little money. One night, I heard a shout in the newsroom. "Well, fellas, the hours may be terrible, but at least the money's lousy." Yeah. Halsey.

Halsey claimed he got interested in baseball at age 11, when his father spanked him when he didn't want to go to a baseball game. "My son will not be a sissy," Dad said. Since then, so the story goes, Halsey was hooked "by the greatest game ever created."

Hall was not a great fan of the obvious. One Sunday morning, he was taking a fishing report over the phone in the newspaper office. The reporter began: "As the sun rose in the east . . ."

Halsey broke in: "Son, if it rose in the west, you'd have a much better story."

The veteran broadcaster hated and feared flying. He didn't endear himself to airline people when he would go up to the ticket counter and say: "One chance to Chicago, please."

And there was the time Halsey got on a plane and promptly fell asleep. When he

ROBERT T SMITH

April 8, 1990

awoke, he asked: "Are we there yet?" The plane hadn't left the ground.

Halsey has been credited with originating the expression "Holy cow" on radio. He said he borrowed it from a catcher named Billy Sullivan. Not long ago, announcers Harry Carey and Phil Rizzuto had a feud over which one of them originated it on air. Halsey had used it since 1919.

It took a strong nose to sit with Halsey in a broadcasting booth for hours. Besides the stogies, he continually ate green onions.

Scott tells of the time his wife unpacked for him after a trip with Halsey. She immediately sent all his clothes to the cleaners and then got on Scott: "I thought you quit smoking. And you tell me you don't like onions."

And no story on Halsey can end without the classic one. Halsey liked his drink and had a habit of carrying a bottle of liquor on trips. A young reporter who had noticed this habit questioned it:

"Halsey, how come you carry a bottle when every hotel has a bar?"

Halsey thought a moment, then said: "My boy, you never know when you're going to run into a local election."

April 8, 1990

She learned to be a friend of Jesus

Each one of us has a cross with our name on it. It is a sign of God's love. We might wish that God had chosen something else—bread and wine, rainbows, the sun. But none of those symbols would be adequate to express the extravagance of God's love for us.

Sister Judy Simon

When Sister Judy Simon died not long ago, there was an obituary in the *Star Tribune*. But I need to add some things to it.

I met her in 1985 when I wrote a column about her. It began:

In 1961, Judy Simon became a Franciscan nun. She lived in a convent, wore the stark, drab habit and didn't speak between night prayers and morning.

Now, she wears blue jeans and jogging shoes, lives in an apartment and spends her days fixing plumbing, changing light switches and, in winter, running a snow blower . . .

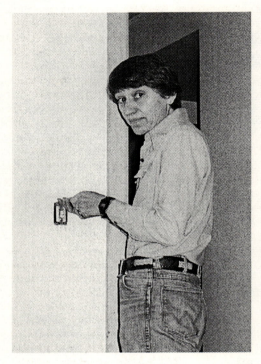

Since then, Judy had spent almost six years in a struggle against cancer. She died, but, in a sense, she won the battle.

Part of that time she helped people build homes in Nicaragua. She wrote a letter in 1988 to her family, friends and relatives. That letter read, in part:

"This trip to Nicaragua is beyond anything I've ever experienced before. Even for things that are familiar, I am tempted to use superlatives: the prettiest sunsets, the most beautiful children's faces, the most brilliant stars . . ."

She allowed as how there also were the hardest labor, the most primitive living conditions and the most insect bites per square inch.

But that was Judy, whose life had both the prettiest sunsets and the most insect bites per square inch. During much of her life, she helped the people of St. Stephen's Catholic Church in Minneapolis, an inner-city parish, racially mixed, with many elderly people. She was the chief janitor there:

"It gave me a spiritual lift to put my hands in the earth. It was a sort of connected-to-the-earth kind of feeling."

And, in terms of the St. Stephen's parishioners, she said:

"I don't give them advice, but sometimes when they need it I give them jobs to make a few bucks. I encourage people not to think they can't do things with their hands."

Judy spent all her life trying to help people. But maybe she helped the most in her attitude toward her cancer. She learned to fight and then to accept her lack of control. Her attitude at first:

"For a long time I was content to be a servant, and not a friend of Jesus. I followed the rules, worked hard, said prayers at the prescribed times, and practiced loving service to others . . . I was keeping Christ at arm's length . . ."

She learned something from the terrible pain of her cancer, in her bone marrow and liver:

"And yet I know that physical pain is often not the hardest suffering to bear. There is the suffering of grief over the death of a loved one, the pain of miscommunication or betrayal by a friend, divorce and separation of families, the feeling of being unloved, the terrible isolation of feeling depressed, or somehow 'different' . . ."

And then there came a revelation for Judy. She learned to be a friend of Jesus:

"I spent about a month recuperating in the Motherhouse infirmary, and it was there that I accepted the fact that I might die soon . . .

"And again, as I always do when I'm in trouble, I turned to God and prayed more frequently . . . It was as if God had said: 'Now that I have your attention, I want you to know how much I love you, and that I am with you.'

"And I got the message over and over again. Sometimes God's love came through in a moment of peace in the midst of anger, frustration and tears.

"It took a while before I could truly say, 'Thy will be done.'

"Many times God's love came in the outpouring of love and support I received from my family and friends, my Franciscan community and this wonderful community of St. Stephen's."

Judy, who once learned Braille to help a blind first-grader at St. Stephen's, was 48 when she died. Her legacy:

"We struggle in the darkness of our suffering and search for meaning in our pain. And there is none—unless we accept the cross and embrace it as a way to intimacy with our God."

For Judy, bread and wine, rainbows, and the sun just didn't do it.

March 30, 1982   **LARRY BATSON**

> **Editor's Note: Robert T. Smith officially retired in 1982, but was persuaded to continue his Sunday column until 1989. The following was written on his official retirement.**

Who needs him? I guess I do.

His desk is clear for the first time since he moved in. For a change, our jointly owned telephone books are where I can reach them, not under layers of debris over on the far corner of his desk. He left some stationery. I'll put that back where he got it: My desk drawer.

When he cleared away the rubble he uncovered some of the copy pencils he was always swiping from me years ago before we started working on computer terminals. He scattered those pencils around the newsroom and the city in lordly fashion, as if flinging coins to the rabble. Big shot.

He always denied taking them. Once I got a fresh supply and carefully bit each one near the end. Left my toothmarks clear as day. He weaseled out of that. Claimed he had been biting his pencils for years.

I won't have to answer his telephone anymore.

The uncertain voices: "Who is this?"

I tell them.

"Well, I wanted to talk to **Robert T. Smith.**"

And a click as they hang up.

There are an awful lot of people whose lives never touch the areas most journalists patrol. They don't make news. They work, pay their bills and draw their pensions or exercise stock options. They raise their families and watch TV. Some swing. Some don't. Some winter in Aspen and Nassau. Some have a favorite place to watch the Aquatennial Parade and they carry their folding chairs down early. These are all Smith's People.

They seldom bother anyone. But other people bother them all the time. With new highways or regulations about painting garages or traffic summonses or new laws about dog leashes. With a thousand changes that they never heard of, don't want, don't feel they need. There are irritants like noise and dumb commercials. Dirty books and X-rated movies sometimes raise the gorge of Smith's people and just as often blue-nosed censors and bull-throated reformers create a royal pain.

Robert's constituency is not confined to the elderly, the infirm or the uninformed and the hurting. Do not make that mistake. Many young people call, professional types, cops, poets.

A lot of them are laughing. There was a wonderful old lady who got an obscene phone call. She was hard of hearing and kept telling the caller to speak up. Eventually, when he was nearly exhausted from shouting, she told him to hang on while she got her husband to take the message.

Many sputter angrily. There was a housewife who had just been taken to jail in handcuffs, she said. For nothing! (Well, as Robert discovered, there had been a little something.)

What Smith's People want is for someone to sort things out and make sense of what is happening. They can handle it, they say, if they can understand it.

Robert generally gets to the bottom of things. He has a knack for turning three pages of bureaucratic hedging, carping and butt-covering into a paragraph of common sense. He has a way of getting people who have almost forgotten how to do it to talk straight.

Robert grew up in this town when cops and citizens still looked each other in the eye when they met. His great gift is the ability to recreate that atmosphere—with old acquaintances or with people he just met.

But why go on? I don't have to take those calls anymore. Because Robert T. doesn't work here anymore.

He won't vanish from sight. He'll write a Sunday column. But officially he has retired. The company made a very handsome

LARRY BATSON

March 30, 1982

offer, as I've mentioned repeatedly, to get rid of him sooner than the rest of us had hoped for.

Smith won't be around every day. And who needs him?

Who needs a guy who rolls into the office—in midafternoon but looking as if he had just dressed in the dark—after you've spent four hours trying to work a piece of writing into something you can abandon without wincing? Who spends the next hour telling you seven funny things that just happened to him. Who leaves the office door open so he can swap wisecracks, insults and gossip with passersby. Who scatters mail from readers, memos from executives and threats from the account-ing department to the four winds—and then calls next day to have you dig through it all and find a name and address he wrote on the back of an envelope. Who somehow, after an hour of raucous disruption, has written his own column and is ready to leave.

Who needs the noise and the needling and a ratty old Greek fishing hat and cigars that smell like sour rope?

Who needs a man who, three or four times a year, without a word being said, cuts off the wisecracks, shuts the office door and looks at you and asks, "What's wrong?"

I guess I do. But a fat lot of good it does me. Smith is leaving.